POETS' GRAMMAR

Also by Francis Berry

Poetry

GOSPEL OF FIRE
SNAKE IN THE MOON
THE IRON CHRIST
FALL OF A TOWER
MURDOCK AND OTHER POEMS
THE GALLOPING CENTAUR: POEMS 1935-1952

Criticism

HERBERT READ

Anthology

AN ANTHOLOGY OF MEDIEVAL POEMS

POETS' GRAMMAR

Person, Time and Mood
in Poetry

by

FRANCIS BERRY

Routledge and Kegan Paul
LONDON

First published 1958
by Routledge & Kegan Paul Ltd.
Broadway House, Carter Lane, E.C.4
Printed in Great Britain
by Butler & Tanner Ltd.,
Frome and London
© Copyright 1958 by Francis Berry

To
INGA-STINA

Preface

PARTS of this book first appeared, in somewhat different form, in *Books, Blackfriars, Essays in Criticism, Notes and Queries* and *Orpheus*. Acknowledgments are due to the editors of these periodicals.

In work of this kind a writer owes almost everything to the help of others, whether he makes use of that help to good or ill effect, and overwhelmingly foremost among those who help him are the dead, but still living, poets and dramatists, aspects of whose grammar forms the subject of this little book. Next to them, he must thank the editors on whose texts of the poets and dramatists he relies, and from which he quotes. The debt is much the largest in the case of early authors and here, especially, I try to acknowledge at the appropriate places the editions I have employed. Also noted in the text are other specific obligations.

There are also those men to be remembered, happily still living, whose thought and writings constitute a major influence. Mr. T. S. Eliot has long exerted such an influence on the present writer who, even when he reacts, as temperament bids him react, against this influence, still realizes that he must be thankful to the origin of the force which inspires reaction. Negative influence, aiding another to discover his own position through the act of dissent, can be as valuable as, or can be more valuable than, positive influence. Perhaps I have not reacted *against* sufficiently.

Next there are those whose conversation, at various times, has provided stimulus, over a period. These are very numerous, but I would especially mention here, and the order is roughly denotative of the order in time of the conversations, Mr. John

Speirs and Professors L. C. Knights, John F. Danby and William Empson. Not that I necessarily expect them to agree with much that follows, nor to like it; nor to agree about it among themselves. In any case they are not responsible for what follows. Yet I owe a good deal, in different ways, to all of them.

But there are two others whom I hold, in some measure, responsible:

Professor G. Wilson Knight, over the many years I have known him, has been a never-failing source of strength and encouragement. On this occasion he may be surprised to find someone, once so wild and unruly, give time to thought over some nice points of grammar. Nevertheless, next to God and myself, I owe it to him that I began to write at all and, having begun, continued.

Fröken Inga-Stina Ekeblad, who is deeply engaged in the study of Elizabethan and Jacobean drama, is above all responsible for this particular book. She shared in the origin of its idea, and then insisted on a book being written, following its progress at every stage and urging it on. An obligation of this nature is only partially met by dedication.

Finally, my thanks are due to my wife for her unceasing devotion in typing and turning all I wrote and re-wrote in the vilest of handwritings into a presentable typescript. Without that sort of practical aid I wouldn't have gone very far.

F. B.

Sheffield

Contents

CONTENTS

I Introductory

I SCOPE OF THE ESSAY

THIS book treats of a few grammatical forms and inflexions as they function in the work of some English poets and dramatists. For this purpose, I am less concerned with the primary meaning of the word Grammar, as given by the *Shorter Oxford Dictionary*, namely "that department of the study of language which deals with its inflexional forms or their equivalents with the rules for employing these correctly", than with that subordinate meaning of the word, as defined by the same dictionary, namely "an individual's manner of using grammatical forms". Just so, except to add that the individuals whose Grammar is to be studied here are poets in the actual exercise of their poetry.

The poems, and their poets, which I have chosen for my task are, in the main, those to which I respond deeply or those which, at any rate, I admire highly. Even so I have had to be extremely selective. For example, two of the greatest of our long poems, *Beowulf* (to no other poem have I responded so deeply) and *Paradise Lost* (no other English poem offers itself to be admired so much) are not even hereafter mentioned: and four other poems to which, along with many others, I owe most—viz: *Sir Gawayne and the Grene Man*, *King Lear*, *The Rime of the Ancient Mariner* and *The Waste Land*—are either not alluded to at all, or but barely and in passing. To investigate the *poetic* function of certain grammatical forms and inflexions in these would take a book in itself. Yet without them, their existence, I would hardly have been encouraged to look at the workings of grammar in other poems.

I

Moreover, I have had to be selective in another way. I have tried to combine the principle of personal response and/or admiration with another principle: that is, that the poems chosen should be representative of all the main phases or 'periods' of English poetry. But not only will it be seen that I have here failed inasmuch as the earliest and the latest (by and large) of these phases are left uncovered, it will also be understood that the two principles are naturally in occasional conflict with each other: hence it is that relatively so much space is given to poets and dramatists of the early seventeenth century, and hence it is that my discussion of three poets in chapter VI is not only brief but unfair. Yet it was right to adopt this second principle and to observe it as faithfully as was compatible with observance with the first. Though this book is certainly not meant to be a history of Grammatical Usage, as illustrated by the poets (the book does anything but claim to be that!), it was still necessary to perceive the variation of *poets'* grammar through the long reaches of our English experience.

Yet my failure to respond very adequately to poems of some periods has had this, possibly beneficial, result. In giving more attention to two (or three) periods than to another, my results show something that a genuine historical survey of grammatical usage might *not* have done—that poets of a period, e.g. Shakespeare, Donne and Tourneur, not only feel the grammatical forms differently but, consequently, use them differently.

As it was necessary to select some poems for investigation in these pages, to the rejection of others, so it was necessary to select certain grammatical forms and inflexions, as they function in the chosen poems, to the neglect of others. English Grammar, we remember, recognizes eight Parts of Speech. Of these eight parts I choose only three—Verb, Pronoun and Preposition. Nor do I include all categories of these Forms. Tense and Mood of the Verb are considered—and only when these figure in positive constructions—but not Voice; and of Pronouns only the Personal, and merely a few of these.

The reasons underlying my choice should be clear from the substance of the book. Meanwhile, of the Verb we can say that this is the Part which communicates all action or suffering; to reflect on the two primary verbs of *to have* and *to be* is to be aware that these two verbs are the instruments for communicating all states of possession and existence: that poetry and drama are concerned with such action, suffering, states of possession and being, and that therefore the behaviour of verbs in different kinds of poetry is of, *prima facie, more* interest than the behaviour of, say, interjections or adverbs. Of the Personal Pronoun, this: here is the one Part of Speech which presupposes human relations and human situations, and if a Personal Pronoun is combined with a Verb to produce such a simple result as *I am* or *He murdered,* one is immediately aware of the impulse behind any lyric or of the action of almost any Shakespearean tragedy—particularly if that 'murdered' be regarded as much metaphorically as literally. As for the Preposition—let its apology await its actual turn in these pages.

While the function in a series of poems of one or other, of both, or of all three Parts of Speech forms the substance of the book, there are two exceptions: my treatment of the fifteenth-century lyric "He bare hym up . . ." and of Shelley's *Ode to the West Wind.* Instead of isolating any particular grammatical elements in these two poems and pointing their function, I have looked at wholes, regarding all Parts of Speech and other elements (rhythm, imagery, etc.) too. This is so because these poems especially invited such an approach—an approach approximating to that of orthodox literary criticism and interpretation. Moreover, I am aware of the possible reproach that in analysing the work of one or two particular elements in a poem I lose sight of the whole, of the subtle interplay of all elements other than the one chosen for analysis. It would be a fair reproach only if the deliberately limited field of my experiment were ignored. Yet, to mark my awareness that the life, however important that life may be of, say, the Verb in a poem is only part of a larger life, I consider two poems in their entireties, though I relate these sections to the subject of the book by an emphasis on the part played by grammatical inflexions in them, a part which has been largely neglected in the study of these poems as in the study of poetry in general.

Here a word might usefully be said on my use of capitals. By 'the Future' I mean the Grammatical Tense, but 'the future' refers to 'time to come'; by 'Subjunctive' the specific Grammatical Mood is intended, but a phrase such as 'subjunctive hopes' alludes to the mood (or state of being) which seems to require the Subjunctive Mood for its verbal expression. This principle has been observed with some consistency, but I am aware that 'time' and 'Time', 'Tense' and 'tense', and even 'verb' and 'Verb', variously occur according to the degree of emphasis, or the shade of meaning, needed by the context.

2   THE MEANING OF GRAMMAR

Now to proceed, for a while, in a less grave tone:

Many of us, remembering the tedious hours spent during schooldays over Kennedy's *Latin Primer* (or even, in undergraduate years, the hours spent over Wright's *Old English Grammar*) might also recall that at that time no other subject seemed so destitute of emotional or imaginative stimulus as Grammar; that no other occupation rivalled in dullness the learning by heart (yet the heart did not enter into it) of declensions or conjugations. Indeed, even until lately I would have contended that the only lasting benefits to be derived from such exercises were a knowledge of the rules governing the mechanics of linguistic expression—a knowledge still, in my case, as must be evident, fumbling and incomplete—and a possession of the rudiments indispensable for an entry into the worlds of the Roman and the Old English literatures. In other words, one learnt Grammar not for its own sake but simply as a *means*. Grammar was dry.

But now I think differently, and for a reason other than a recognition that there is much to be said for the axiom that *any* knowledge is good in itself, independent of whether or no it can be applied for the greater penetration of other knowledge or understanding of life. A pure Grammarian, one who is learned in the historical facts of Grammar and who devotes his time to acquiring more, should indeed command limited respect. Even if he reads Shakespeare for the *sole* purpose of observing, noting, classifying and pronouncing on the grammatical constructions, he deserves, in truth, some esteem. He holds a wealth of knowledge I cannot hope to equal. Yet the real reason for a development of interest in Grammar is quite other than this. The real reason is a growing conviction that in referring the laws—or rules—of language to life we understand more about life (even if that increased understanding of life is but to enlarge the mystery of life) and more about poetry communicating the experience of life.

There is an irremissively active inter-relationship which I like to express thus: language ↔ life ↔ literature. I hope that the double-headed arrows (a needed typographical sign), in place of the normal connective 'dashes', illustrate my meaning, that the current between any two of the terms is not only continuous but two-way. It might be argued that either of the flanking terms could occupy the central place of the formula. It might, but not to the purpose of this book.

What I have said may seem so obvious as to need no saying. Yet is it so obvious? At one university, Eng. Lit. men receive no training in Old English (their experience of English Literature is thereby incomplete and foreshortened) and their lack of interest in the laws of the language is a condition of their ignorance of the language. Now some of these Eng. Lit. men, even those from universities which properly demand some experience of the English fact of *Beowulf* in its only possible form of the English language, are innocents in life. Though the stuff which they have professionally read, and which they professionally teach, is crammed with the experience of lust and sin endured by great Englishmen over thirteen centuries, they themselves have neither sinned nor suffered, though they may yet. But it is often these, who 'apply' to a poem the *ready-made* instruments of the 'New Criticism' and, innocent themselves of vital engagement in language and in life, and therefore innocent of the experience. in the poem—say, *To his Coy Mistress*— pronounce on the poem, a poem which is made *of* language and which grows *from* life. They give verdicts on poems in a manner analogous to a method of marking some examination papers in the U.S.A. The candidates answer the questions on a prepared form on which there are a number of small squares. The candidate shows his knowledge by putting a cross in the right squares out of a much larger number. Meanwhile, a stencil is cut with a number of holes corresponding to the squares which ought to have crosses in them if the candidate is knowledgeable. The examination papers of each candidate are laid rapidly, one after the other, under the stencil and the number of crosses visible quickly calculated. Many of the critics, to whom

I refer, lay a prepared stencil over a poem and, if the crosses do not appear where they ought to appear, the poem is said to fail.

But if many Eng. Lit. men are innocents in language and life, there are—the heavens and we know—many Eng. Lang. men who are the innocents of life and of literature, and who remain so all their lives.

Whether innocence—in language, life, literature (for the inter-relations between these three are, we repeat, irremissively active) is to be lifelong is at the disposal of the temperament of the individual, of chance (perhaps), his will, and of time.

Certainly it is only after a measure of time, long after the grammatical laws of, say, Verb and Pronoun, have been learned by rote—not by heart!—that the mysteries behind, as well as the reasons behind, such laws suggest themselves. Grammatical Tense registers human knowledge of time and its effects (I am . . . I shall be . . . I used to be . . . I was . . . I shall have been . . . I had been . . .) and a knowledge of the truth of Tense can be only derived from experience of time, experience in time. Until one can conjugate beyond the first two Tenses of *amare*, as set out in Kennedy, with an awareness that it reports one's own, and others', chief experience, one has not lived.

Then there is the verb *esse* = to be. The child lives its eternal Present of 'I am'.[1] He may be told of others' past or his own future. Knowing neither, he believes neither. When the child becomes an adolescent he lives *for* and *in* his Future, disdaining his Present and resisting, denying and rebutting his short Past. It is only men or women who have 'had a past', as the idiom significantly has it, those who have conjugated the tenses of *amare*, and therefore the tenses of *esse*, in life, who know the truth of Grammar, and who are likely to refer the grammatical forms in poetry to the experience of their own lives.

And as for *esse* = to be, the verb with Tenses which exist, or can exist, in English or in other languages, as auxiliaries in the formation of the Tenses of all other verbs: the Tenses of *to be* are learned by the Person from the processes of time on his body and from his memory of his body as it *was* in a *past*. Only with,

---

[1] See Blake's *Infant Joy*:
I happy am
Joy is my name . . .

6

and in, time can the Person distinguish his 'I am' from his 'I was'; only with time can he earn his use of these Tenses.

Similarly, it is only with the passage of time, that is only after acquisition of experience (and the main experience acquired is a knowledge of time) that the mysteries of Mood—in contradistinction to the facts of Tense—suggest themselves. Then, at last, the truth of the distinction of *amem* or *sim* from *amo* or *sum*— forms learned with difficulty long ago from Kennedy's right-hand pages, when the question of the truth of the forms did not arise—is perceived—though probably only after the limitations of the Indicative have been known and felt. Whereas the Indicative had become recognized as the Mood of facts, of actuality, of what has been, is, and will be, the Subjunctive Mood comes to signify that which is NOT. It becomes sensed as the Mood of the possible ("It may be that . . ."); of hope ("We may yet . . ."); of despair ("And it might have been but for . . ."); of frustrate desire ("If that we were . . ."); of morality ("We ought not . . ." or " If only we could . . .", the bar here being moral not practical). It is the Mood of that which lies outside time. It is the Mood, then, of the eternal, infinite, absolute: against this, what happens in the Indicative is ineluctably controlled and confined by the physical laws of time and space. As Shakespeare distinguishes:

> This is the monstruositie in love, Lady, that the will is infinite, and the execution confin'd; that the desire is boundlesse and the act a slave to limit—
>
> (*Troilus and Cressida*, III. ii. 78–81)[1]

a sentence implying, from a realization of the friction between two Moods, consequences joyless, tragic, ironic.

But if the Subjunctive is the Mood of that which lies outside time, why is the Latin Subjunctive conjugated in four tenses since tense-time? Yet, as has been suggested to me, the 'time' of the Subjunctive is an unreal time. In our own actual lives we are so time-bound that we transpose our experience of Tense into the categories of the Subjunctive where it does not exist— except with reference to our indicative condition. Thus when

---

[1] Here, and throughout, I quote from the *Nonesuch* edition of Shakespeare, but for *line*-references, not supplied in the *Nonesuch*, I follow the edition of W. A. Neilson and C. J. Hill (Houghton Mifflin, New York).

we say "We might have done so and so", the past *time* of the
deed denoted by this tense is unreal since the deed, in fact,
never took place, and we merely report a no-deed in a no-time.
The 'little ironies' of Hardy's novels arise from the frictions that
develop between 'might-have-been's', never known in time, and
bitter events in the Indicative Tenses.

There are people, we have all met them, who, having found
their subjunctive demands untranslatable into indicative terms,
thereafter renounce the Subjunctive as utterly delusive or unreal.
Such people are active in the indicative business of the world.
There are other people, we do not often meet them, who sheer
away in sensitive terror from the Indicative, deny it all actuality
and so, in the fastness of asylums, believe in their all-sub-
junctive lives as real. It would be presumptuous to attempt to
judge which of these two groups is the braver or more cowardly
of soul. But Shakespeare can help us to realize that when we say
that So-and-so has a 'difficult' life (or an 'interesting' one, come
to that) then the criterion of that 'difficulty' is the degree of
complexity with which the two Moods of half a dozen verbs
carry disputes with each other within So-and-so's heart and
soul. We might also remember that faith, hope and love are
all subjunctive values. The quotation we gave above, from
Troilus and Cressida, confessing the clash between Moods, says
in short what the *whole* play is about, what it says: it says that
the Moods clash. Yet the play does not solve the bitter problem
of the clash between Moods, or determine which of the two is
ultimately real. Troilus' subjunctive hopes are destroyed by
indicative circumstance and so can never become 'real' in the
sense of being translatable into the Indicative Mood (such a
translation always occurring in the Verb-machinery of popular
romantic fiction and fairy-tales). His hopes never enter that
order of time in which a contented present 'is' lapses into a past
'was'—in the sense that some could say "He got what he
wanted and so was content". But how does Shakespeare help
here, or in *Hamlet* where the problem is related, apart from the
help that comes to us simply from his having seen and said the
problem?

While I think that the whole mass of Shakespeare's work
could be fruitfully approached in terms of the tension between
the two Grammatical Moods, all I can claim to offer, in the

appropriate chapter that follows, as a contribution to an analysis of Shakespeare's Moods, are a few notes 'by the way', in the hope that one or two may be taken up and profitably developed by others.

Yet, even despite the shortness of the way I have actually gone in a series of brief chapters, one general conclusion emerges. It is this: Shakespeare's plays and the plays of other Elizabethan and Jacobean dramatists, however charged by the Subjunctive, have a firm hold on the Indicative in a way that few, or no, later plays have. To which it might be answered that poems that are also plays are *bound*, because their main action has to be stage-represented, to the Indicative to a degree which other kinds of poems (for instance Romantic narrative poems) are not, that no other kind of poem requires its substance to be *presently* and visibly enacted. Yet *Death's Jest Book*, almost all subjunctive, exists as a refutation. For it is as much a matter of period as of kind. Not merely the *Satyres* of Donne but also his *Songs and Sonets* have this stand in the Indicative. The Petrarchan Sonnet might have much of the Subjunctive: precisely, but it exists only in reference to—not in reaction against—the Indicative. Behind Shakespeare and Peele, Donne and the English Petrarchan Sonnet, is a medieval respect for the Indicative, a kind of respect which will be absent in, and from, the poetry of the late 1820's, the 1830's, and in most English poetry until 1917.

Yet are we fair to the concept of Mood to say that there are only Two of them? Apart from what Grammarians know, or can deduce, from pre-Ennian Latin, apart from what is known about West Germanic and other extinct or living languages, are we right to assume there are only Two Moods? My chapter on Keats argues that even within the memory of New English a third has been born.

As for the Personal Pronouns—that category of Speech the usage of which, explicit or implicit, is unavoidable in all *human* situations, where two or three (or more) are gathered together, either actual or imagined:

Of all categories of speech it is the one most capable of imposing, or arousing, pain or suffering of feelings, either by deliberate action on the part of the speaker (for to aim to cause pain *is* an action) or by his heedlessness or by his mere ignorance.

9

Capable of being uttered in an almost infinite variety of tones, always according to context, it is the keenest verbal instrument not only for inflicting pain or arousing anger or envy, but it is also the category which—by subtle stress or manipulation—can awaken hope, create joy or communicate love. Of all categories of speech it is the one which, in a human situation, can convey meaning and feeling as much by its omission as its presence. It has a force in silence as in speech.

In the pages that follow I confine myself to a few inflexions of the Second Person—'thou', 'you', 'ye'—as they function in some poems and plays. It is mainly in the first half or so of the book that I concern myself with these forms' function. If, in the second half, my interest in them diminishes, this is no wonder since this reflects a modulation in English life and literature whereby whether a speaker chooses *thou* or *you* in addressing someone ceases to be important only because he ceases to have a choice. He comes to say *you* to anyone or everyone, to one or many. Only in prayers or hymns to God, or in still-being-written-nineteenth-century poetry is *thou* used now. Unless we are genuine and thorough-going dialect speakers (but are there any such?) we English have no verbal instruments, as the Frenchman, German, Swede, etc., still have, whereby we can signalize the passage of a stage in human relations.

Does that matter? Who can say whether the end of *thou* matters, or whether the loss to speech of what is probably the richest word in the Authorized Version does not symptomize an enormous advance in democracy? In poetry, and especially in that species called drama,[1] writers lost, with the loss of *thou*, a primary instrument for denoting the state of a human relation, or a change in that state. We might also remember that the loss of *thou* to, and in, English followed, after about a thousand years, the loss of another Personal Pronoun, WIT. Hence those in love have no word with which to exactly express the joint meaning and feeling of their exclusive society of two members. Donne, as we shall see, has to get round this as best he may.

[1] I am thinking of English drama, 1580–1640, which is poetry. Yet we know the pains William Archer, as translator, takes to explain to his readers, in footnotes, how a person in any Ibsen play changes from being addressed as *De* to *Du*, or *vice versa*.

I might, but for the severe limitations I had set myself, have examined a little of the life of the first Person Plural Pronoun in poetry. Tennyson is the great poet of 'we'. When it is not 'I' with him it is 'we', and he becomes more confident with his *we* as time goes on. Did he share so much with his huge Victorian public that he could feel himself their spokesman? That is for others to consider, for here there is only the space to note that no word is used so frequently, especially in political speeches, but with so much false assumption, dishonesty or self-deception as *we*. Mindful of vertical and horizontal barriers in politics, class, taste and calling, the occasion on which any one of us can say *we* is—an occasion. 'We' are no longer members of one tribe. We, as Englishmen, have no religion. It is the absence of pronominal integers, or the crafty or ironic chariness with which they are used, that marks the 'tribe' now and the literature whispered by those among it who belong only not to belong. Yet Jespersen might have approved. He thought that the English language's defection of inflexions was illustrative of its *practical* advantages over other languages. But even by his test, that a language is good or bad according to the ease with which it can communicate ideas, English has not gained by its losses.

3   POSSIBLE OBJECTIONS

I must attempt to forestall two criticisms. The first is likely to come from the professional linguists.

The linguists may say: You rely too much on Kennedy, and English Grammar is not Latin Grammar despite what Skeat, Sweet and Wright did to make it seem so. They may continue: Grammar was first invented (or devised) for Greek by Alexandrians in the fourth or third century; the Romans applied the categories of these grammarians to their own language; and English students applied Latin categories (though unreal to the spoken language) to Old, Middle and New English, until we lately showed them where they had erred.

But such an objection is fundamentally irrelevant. I am aware that, while there are six Tenses to most Latin verbs, English and all other Germanic languages have only two, Present and Past; that all other tenses, like the Future, have to be rendered by the help of 'auxiliaries'. Yet those other tenses in English or other

Germanic languages, demand, and have ever demanded, forms of expression.

But that is not the point. Even though the categories of Latin (and of Greek) Grammar were transferred to English Grammar, and, though convenient for systematizing Old English, have steadily become less applicable to spoken English, still the basic distinction on which I depend—between Indicative and Subjunctive—holds good. Whatever categories are employed (and, for myself, I think the Continental grammarians' term 'conjunctive' a fairer one than the English and Latin grammarians' term subjunctive, implying *sub*-ordinate value or interest), no one with reason can resist the truth that there is a difference between a Verb Form which states an actual deed or state and that which expresses a deed or state contingent upon the fulfilment of some condition, or which expresses a desire, wish or duty not yet performed or which cannot be performed.

The Classical Grammarians, in fact, perceived their categories to lie in the structure of the mind.

The second criticism I might expect from logicians. To them I would say:

I am *not*, when I talk of Indicative and Subjunctive, merely substituting grammatical terms for the philosophical ones of Appearance and Reality. In the first place, the philosophical terms prejudice the issue. These terms assume an Either/Or; they assume an antinomy; they assume a clear-cut perception of 'a' real as against 'an' apparent which is foreign to Shakespeare and to the rest of English poetry (whatever poets as men may *think*). They postulate a possibly to-be-known distribution between the 'true' and the 'false'. More exactly: they deny the relative degrees of falsehood which the Indicative and the Subjunctive discover as their respective liabilities *vis-à-vis* themselves in the action of a poem such as *King Lear*. Shakespeare did not *know* the Real from the Apparent. Neither did his verbs, but these verbs needed their shifting, and reciprocatingly shifting, doubts and assurances in the room of his poetry. Moreover, we are discussing poetry which is something made out of language out of life, and, therefore, properly use the linguistic terms, and study linguistic inflections, within the limited scope of this essay.

II *Tense in Medieval Pageant and Poem*

I PRELIMINARY

APERSON'S sense of time varies continually during the course of his life. Tenses alter their meanings for him, though perhaps the meaning of the 'Present', the 'Future', the 'Past' successively carry a special emphasis (since young men see visions and old men dream dreams). Moreover, when an adult remembers his childhood two time-scales are invoked: his own now and the one he remembers.

This varying time-scale of an individual's lifetime, his sense of Tense continually altering, reflects the varying time-scales of his society itself in the course of its history, as expressed in its literature. Grammarians have tended to fix categories, which are by definition strict, and yet each period (and each generation within a period) looks on time, and so Tense, differently from its predecessors and successors; and looking on time differently it also apprehends space differently; and, looking on time and space differently, it also regards prepositional relations differently: for example, the significance of *after* (a word of time) and *near* (a word of space) depend on the conception of Tense.

The men of the late middle-ages had their own conception of tense, space and of relations within time and space. One could attempt to define their conception of time and space from an analysis of their world-view or, more inclusive than their world-view, their Dantean view which embraced a future in eternity as well as a now here. Yet more profitably possibly, and nearer to my purpose certainly, we could look at the

Grammar of their plays and poems. From these direct, instead of constructing a scheme, we can learn their conceptions of tense, space and relations.

First we shall consider a case of notorious anachronism, in a Towneley Pageant. After that, instead of focussing on the function of one or two Parts of Speech, we shall study a medieval poem in its entirety, and then draw attention to those grammatical inflexions which make it finally distinct from its nineteenth-century echo or derivative.

2 A TOWNELEY PAGEANT'S SYNTONIC TENSE

In the Towneley 'First Shepherds'' pageant—whose merits are scarcely less interesting than those of the better-known 'Second Shepherds'', as Mr. John Speirs has assured us—the three Shepherds are watching their flocks by night. After much grumbling and grousing against their lot in life, they guzzle an enormous meal. Then they wet their whistles, the homely saying is expressive here, with ale, the "remedy of our woe". This is a formulary used of Christ. Applied to ale it is blasphemously humorous but also strictly apt: the ale makes them forget their troubles, makes them charitably-minded and puts them into the right condition for hearing the impending news of Christ. Cheered up by the drink, they break into song. Next, it is time to gather up the crumbs of the picnic, which are to be given to the poor, and go home. For, the Second Shepherd says:

> It draes nere nyght, . trus, go we to rest;
> I am even redy fryght, . I thynk it the best.
>
> (l. 287)[1]

To which the Third Shepherd replies:

> For ferde we be fryght . a crosse let us kest,
> Cryst crosse, benedyght, . eest and west,
>   For dreede.
> Jesus o'Nazorus,
> *Crucyefixus,*
> Marcus, Andreas,
>   God be our spede!

[1] References are to my edition of the play in the anthology of medieval verse which is included in *The Age of Chaucer* (The Pelican Guide to English Literature, Vol. I).

Immediately following on this advice to cross themselves, and surely the action is suited to the words, an Angel sings, announcing the Nativity of the "lorde perpetuale" who is born "at Bethelem this morne". Yet, it is worth noting, for the sake of what comes, that the *name* of the Infant is not revealed.

The Shepherds are astonished and frightened. The First says:

> I am ferd by Jesus . somewhat be wrang!
> Me thoght,
> Oone scremyd on lowde,
> I suppose it was a clowde,
> In myn ears it sowde,
> By hym that me boght!
> (l. 308)

Gradually, however, they gather their wits together, remember the prophecies in both the sacred Scriptures and in Virgil, and resolve on paying their homage. By the expedient of taking a turn or two about the *pagina*, their stage, they suppose themselves to arrive at "Bedleme". There they offer their gifts—of a "lytylle spruse cofer", suggestive both of treasure and of death; a "balle", an emblem of sovereignty; and a "botelle", possibly a figure for the Chalice, and probably the vessel from which they had lately quaffed their ale—to the Infant.

Now, what are we to make of the temporal confusion to be assumed from this passage? Of the Shepherds crossing themselves? Of their invocation of the blessing and aid of Jesus of Nazareth? Of their familiar knowledge of the crucifixion? Of their ready acquaintance with the names of two of the apostles? It will scarcely suffice to answer that these are simple cases of anachronism such as we find in all medieval literature and art. Moreover, however much, in the work of a medieval playwright, we are accustomed to allow for the unnoticed escape into inappropriate contexts of the signs of his religious faith— signs which a modern writer, with any historical sense at all, would be alert to expunge on revision if he had so much as permitted them to occur—we find ourselves confronted here with examples of what has been called anachronism on a scale and of a kind that cannot be classed as incidental. Nor can they be dismissed as accidental. The 'subject' of the pageant is the Nativity: the announcement of this event to the Shepherds and their response to the news which should, and does, come to them as a great surprise. Surely, it might be argued, a dramatist with any tact would pretend, on behalf of his characters, previous ignorance of the miraculous event whose sudden announcement is so significant? Yet here are characters who show themselves perfectly familiar with that event, and all its consequences, *immediately* before its supernatural disclosure. Not only that: when the news is so imparted, they express wonderment as to what it may mean. That wonder is inconsequent. Nor can we impute the Shepherds' words and actions, and their prior knowledge, to an extraordinary acquaintance with the writings of the prophets (and those of Virgil) or to a detailed clairvoyance of all that was to come to pass, including the method whereby one signs oneself with the sign of the cross. In any case their allusion to the prophets and to Virgil comes later.

As we have said, it is clear that we have to deal with a passage of verse, which is also the turning-point of the drama, in which the 'anachronisms' are not incidental 'escapes' due to carelessness, or to the accident of momentary forgetfulness. Nor is it likely that they owe themselves to a crass ignorance of history— for the most extreme ignorance, as will be apparent, could not explain them. Nor yet is it likely that they are due, for the writer otherwise shows considerable dramatic as well as poetic power, to blundering tactlessness. Rather, we have to recognize that this knot of anachronisms is constructural, basic to the conception and design of the pageant. That being so, we have also to realize that the term 'anachronism', suggestive as it is both of incidental flaw and of accidental error, is inadequate for defining the passage under discussion. The word 'anachronism', and the concept behind 'anachronistic', have taken us a little of the way, but must now be discarded since their further continuance would falsify. Instead, since the passage presupposes some curious conceptions as to the nature of time, structurally inherent in the pageant, it might be better to look at the Verb inflexions, more specially the Tenses, of this—the central passage of the play—since it is these that define ideas of time. In the process we might find ourselves unable to speculate, still less to answer, why the writer of this play conceived of time, by means of his chosen tenses, as he did, but at least we ought to be able to note the mechanics of his tenses and their (to us) strange dramatic and poetic function.

Now, in the first two lines quoted ("It draes nere nyght . . . I thynk it the best") the inflexions of the verbs denote the Present Indicative: A shepherd expresses a fact (the imminence of nightfall) and confesses his resulting state of mind (one of apprehension). He gives reasons for wanting to go home. They are convincing reasons, whether uttered in the person of a Yorkshire shepherd of the fifteenth century or in the person of a Palestine shepherd on the first Christmas eve. The speaker is existing, we might say, either in his own actual present or in the present re-enacted on the stage—the stage-present. More accurately, he is existing in both simultaneously. It might, of course, be argued that most actors at all periods tend to combine the sensation of two lives while actually exercising their calling —their own and that of the person they are representing. But this argument would tend to confuse the obvious truth that on the amateur stage of the Middle Ages—where the three great Cycles of Chester, York and 'Towneley' are concerned, at least —the life, the whole life—not merely the occupational traits— of the players, and of the community of which they were members, was fused with the life and times stage-represented. Some might go further, and urge that medieval players 'saw' other places and periods not 'in terms of' but *as* their own. But this, apart from seeming to insufficiently realize that many of the most venerable crafts and occupations have changed little in their methods through the ages (so that what might be true of sheep-tending or carpentry in the first would also be true in the fifteenth century) is to go too far. Medieval gildsmen would probably recognize a distinction between their own life and times and those of another, but in these plays they would exist in both.

In the lines we have discussed so far, then, there is a con-currence of two Present Tenses: which we will call the Stage-Present (the enacted 'present' of the first Christmas eve) and the Immediate Present (the 'present' of the fifteenth-century actors and audience).

Yet, as the next seven lines (from "For ferde we be fryght" to "God be our spede") reveal, a theory of a 'double tense' does not adequately explain the result, the constructural 'anachronism' of a passage round which the whole play centres. For in these lines we have another set of Present Tenses, now Subjunctive in form, and it is here that the—at first sight—outrageous offence against chronology and the rules of dramatic construction occur, when the Third Shepherd advises that they cross themselves to secure a safe journey home, etc. Hitherto there had been no direct conflict, or contradiction, between the simultaneous Stage- and Immediate Presents but when the Third Shepherd bids his fellows cross themselves, and invokes two of the apostles, then there might appear to be a complete contradiction of the Stage-Present. Yet this denial is not final. For later the Shepherds recollect themselves, as it were. They remember who they are and where they are supposed to be; they enquire among themselves as to the meaning of the angel's message, and they proceed to Bethlehem—so following the temporal order of the Gospels. It may be that we have not experienced the suppression of the Stage-Present at all; rather we have experienced the operations of a third Present Tense, whose virtue enables it to co-exist harmoniously with the other two.

Perhaps we can best approach an understanding of this third Present by reflecting on the different meanings and functions of the two Present Tenses which exist in our modern language and which distinguish English from—say—Latin which has but one Present tense. In fact, the example of Latin will help us to point our case. Latin *amo*, we remember, can be translated into English either as I love *or* I am loving; similarly *rego* as I rule *or* I am ruling, etc. Now when a man says 'I love my country' or 'I love X' he means that his love for his country or for X is a *continuous* state of his being; similarly a government or an idea, if it *rules*, rules continuously as long as it has power to do so. Against these, there is the notion behind 'he is loving' or 'he is ruling'. These denote not continuous states but momentary actions. Further examples multiply. Thus 'she sings' or 'she plays the piano' bespeak that the woman in question possesses the power to exercise these arts—which she could put into practice on occasion; while 'she is singing' or 'playing' means that she is performing particular actions now. Yet while making the distinction it ought to be observed that the

Continuous and Immediate Presents are not necessarily mutually exclusive, even though the meanings of both tenses cannot be expressed simultaneously, or at least so easily, as they can in Latin by the use of the single word *amo* or *regit*.

Now, though the verbs in the lines, where the Third Shepherd blesses himself and remembers the crucifixion and the apostles, appear in a form of the Subjunctive, their meaning is related to that of the Continuous Present ('he loves', etc.) we have been discussing. Related yet not identical. For there is a distinction, marked by the indicative mood of the one and the subjunctive mood of the other respectively, thus: the Continuous Present, though it denotes an unbroken state (while it lasts), envisages a beginning and an end in time—the loving had a beginning and the rule will eventually terminate; the Continuous Subjunctive Present, on the other hand, operates outside—and beyond—time. In the passage from the 'First Shepherds'' pageant, the Jesus who is invoked is not the historical figure whose birth is announced in the temporal context of the Stage-Present, but the eternal Figure of their belief, their eternal 'I am', whose history and whose associates—including Mark and Andrew—existed before their temporal actuality. Thus when the Second Shepherd, near the beginning of the play, addresses the audience with:

> Benste, benste, . be us emang,
> And save alle that I se . here in this thrang!
> He save you and me . overtwhart and endlang,
> That hang on a tre, . I say you no wrang.
> Cryst save us
> From alle myschefys . . .

(l. 46)

he is expressing his own, his fellow-players', and his audience's Continuous Subjunctive Present, the Present of Christ *is* and Christ *saves*, which is a Present Tense that structurally co-exists with the Stage-Present of this history pageant of the Nativity as it also structurally co-exists with the Immediate Present of the players when they rail against the Yorkshire weather or grumble against conditions of labour in the fifteenth century. Whereas a modern Nativity play, performed in some Parish Hall, would offer us players clad in white sheets to simulate Biblical costume, and a dialogue as studiously free of anachronisms as of bawdy humour, the Towneley pageant offered its audience a play that was at once contemporary and 'period' and yet throughout referential to truths that were outside time altogether. It is not a work wherein 'anachronisms' occur but a poetic drama where syntony, or multiplicity of tenses running together, is basic to its conception. The constitution of the psychology of the poet, players and audiences who between them could create and respond to such a work is one which we, with our very different sense of time—and so of tense—would find hard to define or explain. But in the 'First Shepherds' ' pageant we can see its working. If we contrast the Towneley pageant with the contemporary parish-hall type of nativity play (or, even, with much current secular drama), we can begin to understand the authoritative power of verb-syntony, and its advantages, poetic and dramatic, over a conception of time as mere sequence. *There* is flatness; there is dreariness. There is the horror of the limited action; of terminal life.

3 THE GRAMMAR OF TWO POEMS

The quality of a poem depends on the poet's personal qualities —his gift, training, experience, character (and luck). But the quality of the poem also depends on *extra*-personal conditions: on the existence of a tradition in the form he practises, and on the health of the language at the time he writes. The quality of a poem further depends on the presence or absence, and if presence then of its quality, of a philosophy of life (and so of death) of the age and society in which the poem was composed. The quality also depends on the degree of *unconscious* assimilation by society of that philosophy into a mythology: images, symbols, narrative. It depends too on the degree and quality of the poet's engagement in that philosophy and its mythology and the extent to which he can use it poetically. These factors vary from age to age, are constantly varying, but the truth of such propositions can best be illustrated by an analysis of two poems, or rather of two versions of the same poem. The different conditions in two ages account for the profound qualitative difference of the versions and their difference in meaning, whatever their superficial resemblance.[1]

[1] See Appendix I, p. 178.

The first poem is of late medieval composition—probably of the middle-late fifteenth century:

> He bare hym up, he bare hym down,
> —*lully, lulley; lully, lulley*—
> He bare hym in to an orchard browne.
> *The fawcon hath born my make away.*
>
> In that orchard there was an halle,
> —*lully, lulley; lully, lulley*—
> That was hangid with purpill and pall.
> *The fawcon hath born my make away.*
>
> And in that hall there was a bede,
> —*lully, lulley; lully, lulley*—
> Hit was hangid with gold so rede.
> *The fawcon hath born my make away.*
>
> And in that bed there lythe a knyght,
> —*lully, lulley; lully, lulley*—
> His woundes bledyng day and nyght.
> *The fawcon hath born my make away.*
>
> By that bede side kneleth a may,
> —*lully, lulley; lully, lulley*—
> And she wepeth both nyght and day.
> *The fawcon hath born my make away.*
>
> And by that bedde side there stondith a ston
> —*lully, lulley; lully, lulley*—
> *Corpus Christi* wretyn ther on.
> *The fawcon hath born my make away.*

The second was published by James Hogg in 1820:

> The *Herone* flewe eist, the *Herone* flewe weste,
> The *Herone* flewe to the fayir foryste.
> And ther scho sawe ane gudelye bouir,
> Was all kledde ouir with the lille flouir;
> And in that bouir ther was ane bedde,
> With silkine scheites, and welle dune spredde;
> And in thilke bed ther laye ane knichte,
> Hos oundis did bleide beth day and nicghte:
> And by the bedde-syde ther stude ane stene,
> And thereon sate ane leil maydene,
> With silvere nedil, and silkene threde,
> Stemmynge the oundis quhan they did bleide.

A first reading of the first poem, the 'Hill' version (Richard Hill entered it in his Commonplace Book in the early sixteenth century), can leave those people whose sensitivity to poetry is undeveloped fairly unmoved. If the same people follow their 'reading' of 'Hill' with a reading of the Hogg version they are inclined—if pressed for an opinion—to assert the superiority of the latter. But such a judgment usually reflects an ignorance of the conditions attending the making of 'Hill'.

The first poem is a carol. But it is necessary to recover the original meaning of this word 'carol'. The word has been narrowed to denote poems sung at Christmastide in celebration of the Nativity. But the term was once generic and 'Christmas' carols were simply a species. Carols (from the French *carole*) were sung and danced poems. Not until such a poem was *danced* and in being danced sung, was it 'realized', for not until then was it created in the terms of action and sound intended. And 'Hill' possesses the typical form of the carol—namely, two-line stanzas with a double, or alternating, refrain. The stanzas were performed by the leader of the team, while his companions—a chorus—sang and danced the refrain. It is true that, in the case of 'Hill', neither the tune nor the dance steps have survived, and both these must now be inferred from the rhythm of the poem itself and from its character. But a good general description of a carol in performance, though here a Latin carol, is supplied in Robert Mannyng's well-known account of Gerlew and his twelve companions in the churchyard:

> Thys ys the karolle that they sunge,
> As telleth the Latyn tunge;
> '*Equitabat Bueo per silvam frondosam,*
> *Ducebat secuna Merswyndam formosam,*'

with a line of the (probably) double refrain:

> *Quid stamus? cur non imus?*

which Mannyng translates:

> By the leved wode rode Bevolyne,
> With hym he ledde fayre Merswyne.
> *Why stond we? Why go we noght?*

Already we can explain the rhythmic power of 'Hill', in contrast with the Hogg, by reference to its kind and function.

Its heavy accentual beat corresponded to equally definite movements of limbs and body of original performers. But by the time we come to Hogg, the poem was no longer practised as a dance and the stresses, no longer required to define physical movement, were obscured and softened.

There is a relation between function and structure, and the strophic pattern of 'Hill' is to be referred to its purpose. That strophic pattern consists of two lines of a growing 'stem' (that it is a two-lined, and not a four-lined, stanza is evidence of its early date), cross-patterned by a double or alternating refrain. After each of the two lines of the stem, sung by the 'lodesman', or leader, the team, in the form of a ring, danced, and in dancing, sang one of the lines of the double refrain. After the second refrain, 'The Fawcon hath born my make away', there was the 'stand' or pause between stanzas. But, by the time we come to Hogg, the poem is no longer danced, the refrain has no formal purpose, and so has either become lost or merged into the opening pair of lines. In addition, distinction between stanzas has also been lost and the poem has become a piece of continuous narrative verse.

This powerful rhythm of the 'Hill' version is created by many means acting concurrently. There is, to begin with, the definite pause in the exact centre of each line. The insistent balance created by the rhythmic units is much reinforced by mode of syntax. Not only are the grammatical clauses of a standard length throughout, and, with the exception of the first, of a standard structure, but—with the purposeful deviations of first and last stanzas—the two parts of each line, namely adverb phrase and subject and verb, respectively, alternately hold and invert this order, while the rhythmic caesura, coinciding with the syntactical pause, remains constant. Thus (adverb phrase in italics):

> *In that orchard*   there was an halle,
> That was hangid   *with purpill and pall.*
>
> *And in that hall*   there was a bede
> Hit was hangid   *with gold so rede.*
>
> *And in that bed* . . . etc.

This shifting of the two syntactic parts increases, as it cross-patterns, the rhythmic beat (the refrain intervening between each pair of lines) while the one departure, in the last line, from this pattern contributes to the surprise.

Turning to the Hogg version, we observe that the medial pause has either disappeared, or—in the case of the first, second and penultimate lines—remains but in diminished strength. But the loss or submersion of the original syntactical pattern also helps to explain the rhythmic lifelessness of the Hogg. There is no longer a progress of powerfully-hewn, and regularly-constructed phrase lengths, culminating in a line of gigantic effectiveness.

The rhythmic stresses of the first poem are further weighted by massed and massive alliteration. A glance at the poem should suggest the part played by such sounds as those represented by *d*, *p* and *h*. But the sound with the strongest part of all to play is that represented by *b* which runs throughout and acts as a bind. Yet it is not merely a matter of the accumulative force of simply *initial* sounds. There is also the repetition of the series of sounds comprised in the whole words "bare", "orchard", "hall", "bed", and of the whole *phrases* in which these occur. This use of *anaphora*, besides having its rhetorical function (that of insistence towards an end), adds to the rhythmic punctuation. The repetition contributes to another result: it ensures a continuity of meaning which would otherwise have become disrupted through the sheer weight of rhythmic punctuation between stanzas. "Orchard" bridges the gap between stanzas one and two; the word "bed", and its phrase, sets the through-course of stanzas three, four, five and six, despite the violence of a punctuation otherwise divisive.

There is thus a tension between dividing and conjoining forces, a tension from which both parts and the whole gain. The parts gain from that extra definition which they achieve from a momentary isolation as each is delivered in turn; and the whole gains from the use of a device which dissolves isolation and which reintroduces into the meaning of the poem those earlier parts which had apparently spent themselves. In the case of the Hogg version, however, such alliterations and repetitions as survive have the air of accidents that no longer serve any exact, or even limitedly 'rhetorical', purpose.

But if the rhythmic force and personality of 'Hill' contrasts with the rhythmic negativeness of Hogg, so equally does the force, boldness and solidity of the imagery of the one poem contrast with the negativeness, weakness and vagueness of the other—though here it must be said of the 'Hill' that its imagery and rhythm are inseparable save to a purely provisional analysis. Rhythm and imagery do more than support each other. They modify each other. Each becomes in fact an aspect of the other. (In the Hogg, on the other hand, rhythm and imagery are limply co-operative at best.) With this proviso, the best approach to an appraisal of the imagery of the versions comes in fact from an inspection of the adjectives.

Leaving aside the refrain, the versions have the same number of lines. But there is a remarkable disproportion in the number of adjectives between the two. The few adjectives in 'Hill' pull their weight. The many adjectives in the Hogg only fill in lines.

In 'Hill' the adjectives are "browne" (st. 1), and "so rede" (st. 3). There is also "purpill" (a substantive adjective) and "pall" (an adjectival noun). These four have an evident function. The fact that the "orchard" is "browne" corresponds with our own observation of leafless gardens in back-winter (as the period before the first tokens of spring used to be called). Further, "browne" establishes a harmony between the figures and their setting, between nature in its death and the ever-bleeding man and the ever-weeping maid. This harmony is developed in the following lines. For the "purpill and pall", which are the hangings of the hall, invoke the liturgical colours in use in the Church's season of mourning. But if "purpill and pall", being sombre, harmonize with the "browne", they are also splendid and thus have something in common with the "gold *so rede*" of the third stanza. Though this ends the list of *direct* adjectives, there are, in the remaining stanzas, some that are present though muted, such as "rede" which implicitly qualifies the image in "his woundes bledyng". And there are other cases where the reader himself is forced by the poem —because of its dense concretion—to create such qualifications of colour to the visual images. Firm and visually-realized as is the imagery of the 'Hill', it yet acts as the rhythm does, in that individual images for all their success as entities do not exist independently of each other in the final sum. There is a progression of images, and they are no more disjoined from each other than are the rhythmic units of the stanzas. Forceful as they are, no single one presents the poem's movement toward the assault delivered by the surprising and explanatory image of the last line.

Against this, in the Hogg version, the epithets are "fayir" (l. 2), "gudelye" (l. 3), "lille" (l. 4), "silkine" and "welle" (l. 6), "leil" (l. 10), "silvere" and, again, "silkene" (l. 11). Obviously "fayir", "gudelye" and "welle" ('well' equals 'fair' or 'goodly') are simple variants expressive of a general attitude of approval or admiration. Certainly they do not make the "foryst", the "bouir" or the "dune" (equals 'down' or 'plumage') clearer to sight or to any sense. Syllabic-count apart, they could be interchanged without loss or alteration of meaning. The fact that the "maydene" is now "leil" (equals 'little'[1]) is an invitation to the reader to regard her with a patronizing sentimentality. 'Leil', in any case, merely gives the line its complement of syllables, for by 1820 the word 'maiden' had become the romantic designation for any female juvenile below a certain height. Finally, "silkene" (twice) and "silvere" are deliberately pretty. The reader is being asked to adopt a suitable emotion towards a charming, a pathetic, a 'faery', a literary scene.

That the 'Hill' version is the better can be shown by a comparative analysis of imagery and rhythm. Yet the Hogg version has its merits. It is a poem of Fancy—and *is* a fancy of the kind of things which a nineteenth-century reader derived from Spenser. It has melody and charm. The year of its publication also saw the appearance of *La Belle Dame sans Merci*, and, remembering other poems by Keats (and by Scott and Coleridge), Hogg's poem would seem at a glance to be a clear example of the Romantic Revival's interest in fabricating pieces of 'medievalism'.

Actually Hogg's poem is no such thing. Though, in 1820, he printed it as his own work, it is the same poem as the 'Hill' poem, and yet not the same. It is the 'Hill' version after four hundred years of oral transmission, published by Hogg some seventy years before the 'Hill' version was discovered. The changes it has suffered amount to losses which can, in the first place, be referred to a loss of function: the 'Hill' poem was created in the

[1] Though she is perhaps, also, 'leal' = loyal. She is a 'loyal' little person. See *Essays in Criticism*, VI. 3, pp. 361 *et seq.*

living tradition of the *carole*, but, by the time of Hogg, this type of dance-poem was no longer practised and so the poem's formal elements are no longer essentially related to a social purpose.

Above all, in the course of transmission something else has been first weakened, and then completely lost to the poem: its meaning. We have seen that the rhythmic and image units of 'Hill', although having a positive kinetic vitality in themselves, subserve a poetic intention that discovers itself in the last line of the poem. But it is plain that the Hogg version lacks a conclusion. The poem begins at one point of a narrative and breaks off at another, with nothing but arbitrary choice apparently preventing the writer from beginning at an earlier point of the story, or from continuing it in further couplets. Neither his start nor his finish is inevitable. Nor has the poem any real middle. Lines, presenting further decoration or detail, could have been inserted at any one or more places in the course of the version. And in fact a few years earlier, in 1807, Hogg *had* published yet another version in which four additional lines appeared, inserted between the second and third lines of the 1820 version.[1] These lines presumably had no ancestor in 'Hill', but, invented by Hogg, add to the picturesque 'period' charm and perhaps compensate for his abandonment of the sham-antique orthography of the 1807 version.

Hogg's version has no meaning, and when we turn to the 'Hill' version, and ask for *its* meaning, we can give no adequate answer. That is partly because the poem's field of reference has been largely forgotten, but mainly because even at the time of its creation and performance the poem would have seemed mysterious, and its meaning resistant to a translation into intellectual terms, simply because that meaning is a poetic one. There can be no purpose in writing a poem if what it says can be fully conveyed by a prose formulation. The meaning of 'Hill' is both more and other ('other' because 'more') than can be transliterated. But that the 'Hill' version *has* a meaning few would deny; that the Hogg version has no meaning, few would dispute except those who would claim to be able to decipher a palimpsest.

But in attempting simply an approach to the meaning of the

[1] See Edith C. Batho, *The Ettrick Shepherd*, pp. 30–8, and W. Kenneth Richmond, *Poetry and the People*, p. 157.

'Hill' poem, we could begin by temporarily neglecting the refrain and concentrating on the *tableau*. The *tableau* presents the following: a woman kneeling beside a bed on which a knight lies wounded; the bed is richly hung with hangings of ruddy gold; the bed is in a hall which is hung with purple; the hall is in a wood; the trees of the wood are bare of leaves. Actually, these components are perceived in reverse order and lead, finally, to a focus on a stone and an inscription—from which we learn that the knight is Jesus, and the maid Mary. There is also the refrain. Flügel, who first printed the poem, was initially misled by the refrain into thinking that the poem was a secular love lament. It was the poem's final line which caused him to revise this judgment and see the poem as a 'geistliche Allegorie'.

That the 'Hill' version is a *religious* poem is plain. It is equally plain that the Hogg is a secular poem.

But that there is room for confusion within the category 'religious' is suggested by Sidgwick's definition of 'Hill', in 1905, as a *Christmas* carol. In this he was possibly deceived by the points of similarity between it and two versions, taken down in Staffordshire, in 1862, and in Derbyshire, in 1908, respectively.

Theories aiming to elucidate 'Hill', the 'Staffordshire', the 'Derbyshire' and their relationship, have been put forward. Their possible connection with the Graal legend has been hazarded by Miss Annie Gilchrist. In an interesting note[1] she identifies the knight in 'Hill' as Amfortas. He might with equal probability be Malory's King Pellam lying on his bed in the Terre Gaste ('orchard brown'):

And kynge Pellam lay so many yerys sore wounded, and myght never be hole tylle that Galaad the Hawte Prynce heled hym in the queste of the Sankgreall. For in that place was parte of the bloode of oure Lorde Jesu Cryste, which Joseph off Aramathy brought into thys londe. And there hymselff (lay) in that ryche bedde.

(ed. E. Vinaver, i, 85–6)

Though, in any such case, it would mean that the poem's stone with "Corpus Christi wretyn thereon" does not reveal the identity of the knight but rather points to the remedy on whose finding the recovery of the sick knight depends.

[1] *Journal of The Folk-Song Society*, IV (June, 1910).

But, as an alternative to Amfortas, Miss Gilchrist would prefer King Arthur. She has been led to this partly by the reference to the Glastonbury Thorn in the Staffordshire and Derbyshire versions. Here is Arthur (not Jesus) she suggests. He is mortally wounded, lying in Avalon ('apple orchard') awaiting *his* second coming.

If an 'Arthurian' interpretation is secondarily correct but primarily wrong (accepting as the real subject of the poem *Christus mortuus*) then it is because Jesus poetically *includes* these figures of Himself. (Though the reverse does not hold, for none of these *figures* includes Jesus.) Thus: Arthur is a figure of Christ. Like Christ, after *His* death, he is in Paradise, and awaits his second coming when he will claim his kingdom again. Arthur had his knights of the Round Table as Jesus had his company of Apostles; Arthur was betrayed by Mordred as Jesus was by Judas. And so on, but the lesser does not include the greater. That the knight in the 'Hill' version is Jesus and *therefore*, though secondarily, King Arthur (and also King Pellam or Pellas, both or either) need not surprise. For, in 'Hill', the line '*Corpus Christi* wretyn thereon' has a much stronger effect than any allusion to the mode of remedy for any single sick knight, however illustrious, could have. The line, in strict truth, has its shocking power because the stone's inscription reveals the figure on the bed as Jesus. Thereby it also discloses the identity of the 'may' kneeling beside the bed as Mary.

Before I bring some evidence in support of Dr. Batho's contention that the 'Hill' version is a Passion, and not a Christmas carol, whatever the Staffordshire and Derbyshire ones may have lapsed into being, it may not be out of place to refer to the anthropological analogues which a poem, with a subject such as this, is sure to invite, and which must be waylaid however summarily. The difficulty can be broadly stated and broadly answered by saying that even though long before the institution of the Eucharist there were already mystical partakings either of the god himself, or of some sacred food whose effect was regeneration of physical or spiritual vitality, yet that in no way limits the reality or efficacy of the Eucharist. The Graal was not bogus because it had pagan antecedents. We can apply this to our poem and say that because its hinterland includes pagan 'slain god' resources, yet its wealth of Christian reference, especially its reference to pre-Reformation liturgical practice, is none the less real. One should not be forced to vote for the alternative of either a Christian or a pre-Christian interpretation of the poem. In being Christian, the poem is also the other—which is to make it even more compelling as the perspectives, in which allusion can operate, recede.

It was Dr. Batho who first ventured to identify the 'Hill' version as a Passion carol rather than a Christmas carol. I offer now some suggestions in support.

We have noted the poem's use of *anaphora*—the repetition of a word, or series of words, in successive phrases for rhetorical effect. It happens that a similar instance of *anaphora*, and with direct verbal equivalents to what we find in the poem, is found in the Vulgate:

Erat autem in loco, ubi crucifixus est, hortus: et in horto monumentum novum, in quo nondum quisquam positus erat.

This is from the Gospel prescribed for the Good Friday Office in the Roman Rite (viz. *Passio Domini nostri Jesu Christi secundum Joannem*, XVIII, 1–40; XIX, 1–42), and is, of course, the same as that prescribed for the other Rites in Local Use in pre-Reformation England.

The *hortus* of the Gospel corresponds with the "orchard" of 'Hill', and the *monumentum* to the "hall". Both in the poem and in the Gospel passage, someone bears himself—or is borne—to an orchard (garden) and inside the orchard is a hall (or monument, that is Sepulchre). 'Hill' echoes the *anaphora* of the Gospel and intensifies it as the focus is steadily narrowed until we reach the inscription. Additionally, however, the poem seems to refer to a ceremony widely performed on Good Friday during the Middle Ages—that of deposing the Sacrament (v. 'Hill's' *Corpus Christi*) in a Sepulchre, which was a recess in the north wall of a church's sanctuary.[1] A fine, though mutilated, example of a Sepulchre survives at Hawton, Nottinghamshire. This Sepulchre resembles a table-top tomb, on the frontal of which are bas-reliefs of the four sleeping Roman soldiers. On the tomb was placed—on Good Friday—either a crucifix or any effigy of Christ Dead, kept for this annual pur-

[1] See Neil C. Brooks, 'The Sepulchrum Christi and its Ceremonies in Late Medieval and Modern Times', *J.E.G.P.*, XXVII, April, 1928.

pose. On the wall of the recess above this frontal is a carving of Christ Resurrected (the spear-wound in the *right* breast and the blood-flow realistically shown). There are other carvings of Mary and of angels. On the left of this recess there is the further excavation of a small cell for the deposition of the Sacrament on Good Friday on which occasion the Sepulchre generally, including especially the entry to the innermost recess, was richly decorated with hangings denoting regality and mourning.[1]

Now one is not concerned to make this suggestion—drawn from Church architecture and liturgical history—carry more than it can fairly bear. But light is thrown, perhaps, on the 'Hill' poem to this extent: At the time of the poem's composition events recounted by St. John in XVIII, XIX, and also, equally, by the imagery of the 'Hill' poem (in its full *ensemble* of "orchard", "halle", hangings, "bede", "knyght", "may" and "*Corpus Christi*"), were represented in tableau form in churches on Good Fridays.

And this conclusion yields one result to the literary critic. If 'Hill's' formal vitality is to be at least partially related to its contemporary social function (the poem was intended to be danced and sung, and was written in a living *carole* tradition), then the vitality of its substance of imagery is also to be related to the background of experience—shared by poet, performers and audience—derived from a religious practice popularly observed. Further, one can indicate the quality of both the collective background experience and of the poem's imagery by the observation that it was in this particular religious practice that the precepts of Catholic faith and the human emotions of awe and pity combined to the fullest degree.

All this goes to explain the frailty of Hogg's secular version. As its form has lost the justification of a served function, so has its imagery become detached from a tradition of belief and practice. Hence the knight has shrunk into an anonymous knight, and the 'may' has also certainly dwindled. The suffering of the one and the action of the other have lost significance. Not that the few critical judgments on 'Hill' have all been favourable. Sir Edmund Chambers, for example, does not 'see anything in it (except the May's grief for her Son) imaginatively rendered' (*English Literature at the Close of the Middle Ages,*

[1] See J. Charles Coxe and Alfred Harvey, *English Church Furniture.*

p. 112); while A. H. Bullen thought its interest solely historical (*Notes and Queries*, 1905, iv, 181). On the other hand Dr. Batho implies a high regard (*The Ettrick Shepherd*, p. 32); also Mr. Kenneth Richmond, in a brief though stimulating comparison between the versions (to which I acknowledge an indebtedness), expressly states his admiration (*Poetry and the People*, p. 4).

But apart from—yet related to—his other advantages, it must be admitted that the language enjoyed by the writer of 'Hill' was superior to that at the disposal of the Ettrick Shepherd. The language—in which, with which, and *through* which both poets worked—was, for the writer of 'Hill', much more robust, and was much more a part of the somatic, as well as mental, life of those who spoke it than it was for Hogg. This was so even despite the fact that James Hogg came of a breed which had immemorially lived in a remote part of Scotland, following an ancestral economy, in which the youthful Hogg had his place as a shepherd. This community was mainly illiterate— hearing and knowing a word instead of simply seeing it. (And indeed we should bear in mind throughout this discussion that it was an illiterate, Hogg's mother, who was responsible for her son's versions. Hogg simply wrote down—except perhaps lines 3–6 of the 1807 version—what his mother had said or sung to him as a child.)

The fact that by 1820 Hogg had become, to Mr. Richmond's disgust, a *literary* man of polite Edinburgh, deserting his ver- nacular (and all that that implies), is therefore irrelevant. Nevertheless, a comparison between the two versions has shown that the vernacular of Hogg's community was a poorer instrument to handle. In general, its weight and texture is thinner and lighter. The words as sounds are less sonorous and they signify less. Even when the words *appear* identical with 'Hill's' they are not the same because they have shed some, or much, emotional and intellectual experience. And it is not that their denotation has become sharper as their connotative power has diminished. It is true that if they had been more apprecia- tively handled, some of their lost ancestral emotional and intellectual content might have been re-created through rhyth- mical means. But then only partially. It is a case of recognizing that the language, from around 1660, while becoming, as

Mr. Eliot has said 'more refined', certainly lighter, quicker, has become thinner and less interesting because of its severance from much valid experience of the remoter English past.

Any number of theories can be advanced to account for this thinning, which the minority sensitive to language can in any case feel. Mr. Richmond, for his part, stresses the effects on the language that have resulted from its speakers having gradually become urban dwellers, combined with the fact that the production (and so consumption) of literature has become the concern of a learned or polite *caste*. Certainly, with the destruction of the village, where individuals, their ancestors and descendants too, had lived together, had been bound together by continuous economic and emotional relationships, came the end of the only kind of organic society (which was also a figure of mankind in its diversity of sex, age and occupation) which the human being has so far been able to comprehend emotionally.

Such a society, and such an experience, necessarily enjoins a consideration of a theory of language such as that of Sir Richard Paget's. When spoken language was an unconscious vocal mimetic re-creation of the matter it communicated (i.e. when objects were directly apprehended in the utterance of their names, when actions were muscularly reproduced in the saying of verbs, and when the speaker's attitudes to his re-creation was expressed by epithets born of a direct physical—as well as mental—reaction), then that language had directness and immediacy—it transmitted experience as well as rational meaning. That experience would, to the modern mind, appear to have been narrow, however intense. It would appear to have been the experience of small societies of agrarian or pastoral life, confined to a locality much subject to the operations, often malign, of a Nature of which they were acutely aware.

This is possibly true. But, with its extended intellectual sympathies, the modern mind has not only failed to extend its imaginative sympathies but has lost such local sympathy as it once had. The thinning of the language is the evidence for this loss. This is sufficient evidence for a sufficient loss.

Consider the opening line of 'Hill's':

He bare hym up, he bare hym down,

as an example of what Yeats called 'blood, intellect and

imagination running together'. And remember that the movements of the thrusting verbs were not only re-created orally, but that they were simultaneously re-created by the movements of the body of dancers who were thus

> Keeping time,
> Keeping the rhythm in their dancing
> As in their living in the living seasons
> The time of the seasons and the constellations
> The time of milking and the time of harvest
> The time of the coupling of man and woman
> And that of beasts.[1]

Thus the harmony in 'Hill', between the figures of "knyght" and "may" and their background of the "orchard browne", asserts an unconscious harmony between man and the rest of God's creation—Nature, however localized in its workings.

This harmony disappears in the poetry of Hogg's version. So does the relationship between the 'knichte' and 'maydene' and the rest of humanity. This latter bond is, in 'Hill', established by that refrain which had once led Sidgwick to suppose the poem a secular love-lament. It is, indeed, of the kind that we might expect to appear in any folk-song whose subject is a widowed mother lulling a child to sleep. For the "fawcon", which can also strike the small animals, is as clearly death, as the "Herone" is no-one in particular outside itself. Thus 'Hill', by stanza and refrain, alternately contemplates the death of Christ and the connection between this death and bereavement as a part of common experience.

This brings us to the consideration of that which is the supreme guarantee of 'Hill' as a poem. More necessary even, as an explanation of the poem's authenticity, than the postulate of a society living *en rapport* with Nature and with the kind of language that arises from this, is the recognition of the poetic efficacy of religious belief. For it is the poet's belief in the figure in the hall as Christ as well as knight, as a divine Person, who is dispensing in eternity while immediately dead in the tomb, that gives the poem an unlimited reverberation of significance such as the Hogg version cannot even begin to claim. And the belief of the writer was the belief of his society, and of the performers of the dance. This belief, with its contingent emotional

---

[1] T. S. Eliot, *East Coker*.

and intellectual patterns, existed, of course, before this poem, and merely awaited a special vitalization through the means of the particular organization that is this poem. In contrast, Hogg could depend on no such co-operation from his readers; nor could he presume on the power of their memories. Moreover, in alluding to the intellectual patterns contingent on belief, we recall that medieval Christianity not only controlled vast resources of feeling in its forms of devotional patterns, but that it controlled a philosophy which demonstrated Nature's participation in human destiny. Hence the "orchard browne" of the 'Hill' poem is more than a setting. It is responsive to the emotions of "knyght" and "may", and it continues to participate in their sufferings.

As promised in the Introductory Chapter and in the first section of this Chapter, we have taken an opportunity to consider the function of the grammatical forms and inflexions in a short poem—or in two poems—not in their isolation, but in what has been called 'the total semantic complex' (a term quite incomplete unless it is held to include the sound—or phonal—qualities, which qualities are wholly at one with the semantic in the 'Hill').

To our particular observations on the adjectives, on the pronouns (the 'he' of the 'Hill' version becoming the Christ of its last line; the identity of the 'knichte' and 'maydene' of Hogg remaining anonymous since their identity does not matter) and on the formal syntactical arrangement, we must add a note on the verbs. As with the Swedish *visa* discussed in chapter X[1] we should note that the dialogue or tension between 'stems' and refrain of the 'Hill' poem is a dialogue *and* tension between the two kinds of Tense. The dominant Tense of the stem is the Present. Nor is it the Historic Present. Though Christ died in the past, yet His Passion is being *presently* revived with the performance of the carol. Against the dominant Tense of the stem is set the Tense of the refrain. In the words 'The fawcon *hath* born my make away'[2] the team, or chorus, answer to the lodesman's present story of Christ's Passion by referring it to their—and all women's—suffering, though their loss of a 'make' is, like all experience, necessarily set in the past.

[1] See p. 169.   [2] Italics mine.

III Pronoun and Verb
in Shakespeare

I 'THOU' AND 'YOU' IN THE 'SONNETS'
IN RELATION TO TENSE

IN his *Sonnets* Shakespeare sometimes addresses the young man whom he loves as 'thou' and at other times as 'you'. Each term governs a correct sequence of oblique cases and possessives: thus 'thee', 'thy', 'thine' agree with 'thou'; 'your' and 'yours' agree with 'you'.

The 'thou'-sonnets, according to the 1609 Quarto numbering, are:

> 1–12; 14; 18–20; 22; 24; 26–32; 34–51; 56; 60–2; 69–70; 73; 77–9; 82–93; 99–101; 107–10; 122; 125–6; 128.

(Altogether 73 sonnets.)

The following are the sonnets wherein he addresses the young man as 'you':

> 13; 15–17; 24; 52–4; 55; 57–9; 71–2; 80–1; 83–6; 98; 102; 104; 106; 112–15; 117–18; 120.

(Altogether 37 sonnets. Note that the last 'you' in the series occurs in sonnet 120. Also note that sonnet number 24 appears in both lists.)

It will also be seen that there are almost exactly twice as many 'thou'-sonnets as there are 'you'-sonnets: that is, among those addressed to, or dealing with, the young man—which are the ones I shall mainly discuss. Yet, the proportion of 'thou'

sonnets, with regard to the *whole* sequence of one hundred and
fifty-four is even larger, for the conventionally-termed 'Dark
Lady' is always addressed as 'thou', never as 'you'. The sonnets
where she is so addressed are:

133–7; 139–43; 149–50; 152.
(Altogether 13 sonnets.)

Now, the question: What is the difference, in *poetic* result,
between a 'thou'-sonnet and a 'you'-sonnet? Or, to put it in
another way: What was the reason, conscious or otherwise,
which induced Shakespeare, whenever an instant of need arose,
to use—since the choice existed for him as it does not for us,
for us 'you' must serve all purposes irrespective of number—
this pronoun rather than *that* pronoun?

The distribution, throughout the sequence, of the two forms
shows, I think, that his choice is not to be explained in such
terms as that he uses 'thou' for his more 'Petrarchan', imma-
ture, or conventional, style; and the 'you' for those sonnets in
a more colloquial, mature, or Donne-like style. For, in this connection, it should be said at once that Donne (*a*) is unique
among English poets in that the bulk of his work centres around
a two-person relationship; himself and a mistress in *Songs and
Sonets*, himself and God in the Divine Poems; and (*b*) that,
in this relationship, Donne habitually speaks to the other—
mistress or God—as 'thou'.[1] Neither could it be maintained,
assuming (as the overall stylistic development warrants)[2] that
the sonnets were printed, if not in their exact, at least in their
approximate, chronological order of composition, that the distribution of the two pronominal forms *only* reflects a general
linguistic change over the years in which the sonnets were
written. We would, if that had been the case, have expected
the 'thou's' at the beginning, and the 'you's' at the end, of the
series of sonnets. But this is not so. Nor, for this and related
reasons, can it be held that E. A. Abbott's statement, "*Thou*

---

[1] For, it will be seen that 'you' in Donne almost exclusively denotes a
plural—explicit or implicit. (In the Divine Poems 'Thou' is God the Father,
but 'you', in a poem addressed to the Trinity, is the 'three-personed' God.)

[2] I speak for my own feelings when I say the overall stylistic development
warrants the assumption; but I am well aware that the matter of the
chronology of Shakespeare's *Sonnets* is a highly controversial one.

in Shakespeare's time was, very much like *du* now among the Germans, the pronoun of (i) affection between friends, (ii) good-humoured superiority to servants, and (iii) contempt or anger to strangers", adequately explains the distribution of the two forms in the *Sonnets*, despite the support it receives in the pages of W. Franz's *Shakespeare-Grammatik*. Abbott also says that 'thou' having "already fallen somewhat into disuse, and, being regarded as archaic, was naturally adopted in the higher poetic style and in the language of solemn prayer". But this does something worse than beg the question. What is the 'higher style'? Why should Shakespeare use it in sonnet 56 but not in 57? The style of one is not noticeably 'higher' than the style of the other. What is applicable to nineteenth-century poetry or to hymns is obviously out of place here.

Now, additional to any special local needs of rhyme or euphony, we would expect Shakespeare to choose, not at random, but meaningfully and sensitively. We can, in other words, expect some significance in the fact that one sonnet may be built around an 'I-thou' relationship, while another sonnet centres around an 'I-you' relationship. Now, this is exactly what we find: for while within the 'I-thou' relationship there is a great variety of states as, equally, there is within the 'I-you' relationship, yet the two—the 'I-thou' and the 'I-you' relationships—never coincide and they are distinguished by the pronominal forms employed. The person addressed as 'thou' is conceived of differently from the person addressed as 'you', and this further implies that Shakespeare himself (the 'I' of both sets of relationships) also changes according to the pronoun he uses.

Sonnets 1 to 12 are 'thou', or 'I' to 'thou', sonnets:

> But thou contracted to thine owne bright eyes,
> Feed'st thy lights flame with selfe-substantiall fewell,
>
> Thy selfe thy foe, to thy sweet selfe too cruell:
>
> (1)

and:

> Looke in thy glasse and tell the face thou vewest,
>
> (3)

and:

> .   .   .   .
> In thee thy summer ere thou be distil'd:
> .   .   .   .
>
> (6)

and:

> .   .   .   .
> So thou, thy selfe out-going in thy noon:
>
> (7)

and:

> As fast as thou shalt wane so fast thou grow'st,
> .   .   .   .
>
> (11)

to give a few examples of address. Here the 'I' (Shakespeare)
beholds; the 'I' worships; the 'I' delicately admonishes the
superb and lovely 'thou'. But the beautiful 'thou' is remote,
is a shape of youth, is seen but not heard, is seen but not
touched or felt, is distant not nearby. The images are visual
and yet distant, thus:

> ... beauties *Rose* ... (1)
>
> Thou art thy mothers glasse and she in thee
> Calls back the lovely Aprill of her prime,   (3)
>
> Loe in the Orient when the gracious light,
> Lifts up his burning head, each under eye
> Doth homage to his new appearing sight,   (7)
>
> ... summers green ...   (12)

The melodies in which these images descant are beautiful,
tender, melancholy-sweet, though the sun shines and the light
is high. The distance or range between the 'thou' and the 'I'
is not elastically variable, but—vaguely far—is a constant. The
tone of address is another constant. The mood of adoration is
a constant. The 'thou' so loved, apart from, or within or behind, his enchanting shape and grace (though it would be a
pity to see him die without issue) is an unknown to the 'I', or
to us, the readers. It might be said that sonnets 1–12[1] express
Platonic or ideal love, or the first phase of an emotion which,
of all emotions, has its recognized phases. Certainly, because

[1] No. 5 is unique in this group in being devoid of any pronoun of the
second person. But the absence is apparent only: it is addressed to an
assumed 'thou'.

the 'thou' is as yet so unknown to the captivated 'I', the 'I' does not know what this Love has done to him. So the new 'I' is also unknown. The pronoun chosen betokens distant admiration in these sonnets, and though the effect of Time on Beauty is their professed theme (so the adored one had better hurry up and marry), it is not their real theme—first, because Time, though blamed, is not apprehended as destructive; and secondly, because it is only this professed 'theme' which gives Shakespeare the happy excuse for addressing the youth at all. Time must be thanked, for: "hurry up and marry (as others are all saying) because Time will take its revenges" simply provides an opportunity for the 'I' to write to 'thou'. Moreover the lovely youth is too far away to be truly destroyed by Time, and so Time's work is the ostensible theme only. Yet, when the theme is not ostensible but real, it is of all themes the one likely to force a writer's uneasy and disturbing contemplation— necessarily uneasy and disturbing—of past, present and future; of a Present Time which will become the Past, of a Future which will become first Present and then Past. Such a contemplation does become the heart of the matter of the greatest sonnets—those between 57 and 71—in which the poet *realizes* that "time that gave, doth now his gift confound" (60).[1] In these sonnets—majestic, most intense—which form the centre of gravity of the whole sequence, the Tenses do ring the changes of their conjugation. But in 1 to 12, within the frame of those platonic constants in which they have their being and where the primary theme, within a frame of platonic constants, is 'I adore thee', and where the warning 'Beware time', however stated as primary, provides merely the excuse for address, the actual grammatical Tense is predominantly the Present (Active or Passive) Indicative, while the underlying, *poetic* Tense is everywhere a kind of Continuous Present.

Here I should say that I do not consider 1 to 12 inferior to the others for being what they are, nor do I rate the first phase of love, an extraordinary admiration, lower than any succeeding phase. Also, at this stage, to avoid misunderstanding, we are compelled to say this: the 'thou' of 1 to 12 does not mean that its appearance in Shakespeare, or in other writers

[1] See L. C. Knights' study of the Sonnets in *Explorations*.

of the time, *necessarily* implies a worshipping regard with simply
a hope, or not even that, of its being reciprocated. In 1 to 12
it does indeed betoken a worshipping regard; but the 'thou'
in the sonnets addressed to the Dark Lady betokens, as we
shall see later, a degree of contempt. There Shakespeare half
despises himself for being enslaved to her charms. Yet Antony
as a rule addresses Cleopatra as 'thou'; Romeo addresses
Juliet—as he does Death, etc.—as 'thou'; and Donne (as we
have said before) consistently uses 'thou'. Basically, the word
—and the relation 'I-thou'—implies division, duality, two-
dom, separation of entities. This sense of division is necessary
for drama (where the persons must be seen to be distinct), and
was necessary for a person as domineering, masculine and
'separate' as Donne. But in the Sonnets, *degrees* of separation
and union are expressed, and here the alternative pronouns
'thou/you' are instruments expressive of these degrees as felt
by Shakespeare and experienced in the poems. Not only degrees
are expressed, levels too. When Shakespeare uses 'thou' to the
Fair Youth, he looks not only afar off, but upwards. He hopes
he will be heard; he does not presume to hope he will be
answered. But, when he uses 'thou' (as he always does) to the
Dark Lady, he condescends. He does not care whether she
listens and, probably, would prefer not to have her answer.
When 'you' is used, there is some equality, some background
of give-and-take.

It is in 13 that 'you' (along with 'your', 'yours', 'yourself')
first appears:

> O that you were your selfe, but love you are
> No longer yours, then you your selfe here live,
> Against this cunning end you should prepare,
> And your sweet semblance to some other give.
> So should that beauty which you hold in lease
> Find no determination, then you were
> Your selfe again after your selfes decease,
> When your sweet issue your sweet forme should beare.
> Who lets so faire a house fall to decay,
> Which husbandry in honour might uphold,
> Against the stormy gusts of winters day
> And barren rage of deaths eternall cold?
> O none but unthrifts, deare my love you know,
> You had a Father, let your Son say so.

It makes an exciting innovation—and it makes the poem. Substitute, for the innovation, the previous 'thou', 'thine', 'thyself' ('and/ thy/ sweet semblance to some other give', etc.) and the sonnet is one with the first dozen; but the effect of 'you', 'yours', 'yourself', in this context, is to shorten the range of address. The youth is seen in a new perspective—or not seen, for his you-ness is *sensed*, apprehended—in such a way that the advice is intrusive, nearly impudent: Shakespeare is closer, is being 'familiar', is risking 'freshness'. Yet it is the 'you', 'yours', 'yourself' alone that work this, for glance through the sonnet and the rest of its diction is seen to be of the same character as that of 1 to 12, and its Subjunctives but the aspirations within Mood of a Continuous Present.

'You' is, then, more intimate, 'thou' more formal—the opposite of what might be expected according to some imaginary Elizabethan Fowler of Correct Usage. But the plural form has another poetic effect. For in

> O that you were your selfe, but love you are
> No longer yours, then you your selfe here live,

the one previously saluted as 'thou' and a unity, has become a compound of body and soul, where the body can betray the soul's will or wish. Through the plural form a sense of duality is broached in the poetry.

But the daring poetic experiment of 'you' was not matched by the rest of the diction ("when your sweet issue your sweet forme should beare", etc.), and in 14 Shakespeare *reverts* to 'thou'; then ventures in 15 on 'you' again, but with a much more massive accompaniment of suitable 'you' diction and thought. As hitherto, it is officially about Time, but now it exploits Tense more knowingly so as to realize the subject. The whole sonnet is built on a Time-thinking, expressed through the scheme of 'when'-clauses followed by the saturnine 'then'-clause: the body of the 'you' addressed is part of a whole structure of matter that waxes but to wane. But the part is a plurality; it has a soul. After 15 the poet relapses once more to 'thou', and continues to work out the 'I'—'thou' and 'thou'—'I' relation, until he reaches the powerful squad of sonnets 44–62 where 'thou' and 'you' alternate, but alternate significantly. Of 47–62, an appropriate epigraph summing the basis of the distinction between 'thou' and 'you' might be proposed:

> Betwixt mine eye and heart a league is tooke,
> And each doth good turnes now unto the other,
> When that mine eye is famisht for a looke,
> Or heart in love with sighes himselfe doth smother;
> With my loves picture then my eye doth feast,
> And to the painted banquet bids my heart:
> An other time mine eye is my hearts guest,
> And in his thoughts of love doth share a part.
>
> (47)

Yet before that charged load of intensity—the heart of the series—is reached, there is the engaging queerness of 24 where both pronominal forms are encountered. But here the shift in l. 6 from 'thy' to 'your' is due to a shift on the 'I's (Shakespeare's) part *into* the 'thou' where Shakespeare sees as from his ('you's') point of view.[1] 24 is more of a gay game than most of the sonnets; it marks a phase of love, and the swopping—pretended or assumed—or blending of eyes, hearts, etc., is as much part of the game as the swopping or interchanging of pronouns.

In the series 49–62 the 'thou' and 'you', as we have said, alternate, and develop their separate significations: significations that seem to correspond to the opposing claims of eye and heart, as in 46:

> Mine eye and heart are at a mortall warre,
> How to devide the conquest of thy sight.

Yet these lines do not fully define the difference lying behind the two pronouns. Consider the kind of context where 'thou', 'thee', 'thy' or 'thine' is used:

> Against that time (if ever that time come)
> When I shall see *thee* frowne on my defects,
>
> .   .   .   .
>
> Against that time when *thou* shalt strangely passe,
> And scarcely greete *me*. . . .[2]
>
> (49)

---

[1] A reading I owe to Inga-Stina Ekeblad.

[2] Here and elsewhere the italics, when additional to those marked in the Quarto, are my own.

or:

> Thus can my love excuse the slow offence,
> Of my dull bearer, when from *thee* I speed,
> From where *thou* art, why should I hast *me* hence,
>
> (51)

as against the kind of context where Shakespeare chose 'you':

> So is the time that keepes *you* as my chest,
>
> (52)

> What is *your* substance, whereof are *you* made,
>
> (53)

> Nor *Mars* his sword, nor warres quick fire shall burne:
> The living record of *your* memory.
>
> (55)

> Being *your* slave . . .
>
> (57)

> Be where *you* list, . . .
>
> (58)

If we sound the two uses carefully, we find—without pressing the matter too far—this kind of difference between 'I-thou' and 'I-you': When Shakespeare uses 'thou' in these central sonnets, there is a measure of self-regard and self-pity. He is thinking as much of himself as of the youth. Nevertheless the 'thou' is seen as a kind of fate, as an obdurate 'fact' in the stream of his—Shakespeare's—life. The 'thou' is something that has befallen him and which may or will (the Future Tense threatens—see the above quotation from 49—it does not offer hope) desert him.

The 'you' is more of a person—a suffering, wilful, flesh-and-blood, soul and body, person—and the 'I' who addresses him is then less the poet who will confer immortality than an ageing man—another *person*—and the 'I-you' relation is something then seen more humourously, more wrily, more honestly, more pathetically than is possible within the *immutable* 'I-thou-perspective.

Now I suggest that it is through the 'I-you' approach that

Shakespeare reaches the stance of spirit assumed in the series
64–68 inclusive—that tremendous block of poems where the
youth has passed through from being a 'thou' or 'thee', has
overpassed even the status of being a 'you', and has become a
'he' or 'him', earning the designation of the Third Person
Singular. He is seen or sensed objectively as a tiny figure—he
seems to have shrunk—and he too is a victim (the most precious
victim) of Mutability:

> Against my *love* shall be as I am now
> With times injurious hand crusht and ore-worne,
> When houres have dreind *his* blood and fild *his* brow
> With lines and wrincles . . .
>
> (63)

> Shall *times best Jewell* from times chest lie hid?
>
> (65)

> Why should *he* live, now nature banckrout is,
>
> (67)

> Thus is *his* cheeke the map of daies out-worne,
>
> (68)

In seeing the youth objectively as *he* is, and as Shakespeare
knows himself to be, a subject of Time, the writer at least has
achieved a kind of mastery: knowledge of the *situation* in which
both exist.

That the later sonnets return to 'I-thou' or 'I-you' is natural
enough. Shakespeare now knows that "you alone are you" (84)
so that 'thou', when applied to the 'fair youth', is used with a
new self-consciousness. When it is applied to the Dark Lady,
then it is used with a wide range of overtones in which self-
disgust and bitterness are prominent:

> Me from my selfe thy cruell eye hath taken,
> And my next selfe thou harder hast ingrossed.
>
> (133)

> Be wise as thou art cruell, do not presse
> My toung-tide patience with too much disdain.
>
> (140)

In loving thee thou know'st I am forsworne,

· · · · · · · ·

And all my honest faith in thee is lost,

(152)

for she, like the Rival Poet, was also bound for the prize "of all too precious *you*", (86) and while in Shakespeare's arms was still remote from his affections.

Our main purpose has been the consideration of Pronouns, but we will conclude with a note on Tense in the *Sonnets*. We have seen that when the one Shakespeare loved turned from being a 'thou' to being a 'you'—became a being with a mortal body and a fallible soul—that it was then that Shakespeare became urgently Time-aware, and so Tense-conscious. With the use of 'you' the original 'Continuous Present' of the (especially earlier) 'thou'-sonnets became ruffled, broken-up, chopped into Imperfect, Pluperfect, Future, etc. And this process becomes even more marked, perhaps, in those sonnets where Shakespeare—viewing his situation from outside as well as suffering within it—could see the Youth (and sometimes himself too) as a Third Person to be styled 'he'. Observe, for instance, the variety of Tense, Voice and Participle in:

> Against my love *shall be* as I am now
> With times injurious hand *crusht* and *ore-worne*,
> When houres *have dreind* his blood and *fild* his brow
> With lines and wrincles, · · · ·
>
> · · · · · · · ·
>
> And all those beauties whereof *now he's* King
> *Are vanishing*, or *vanisht* · · · ·
> *Stealing* away · · · · ·
> For such a time *do I now fortifie*
>
> · · · · · · ·
>
> That he *shall never cut* from memory
>
> · · · · · · ·
>
> His beautie *shall* · · *be seene*,
> And they *shall live*, and he in them still greene.

(63)

It is just such friction between the sadness of the actual meaning of the verbs and the decoying melody to which they are set which creates that distinctive bitter-sweet flavour of not only certain well-known passages of *Love's Labour's Lost* or *Twelfth Night*, but of these plays as wholes.

But for a harsher and more ranging apprehension of Time, and therefore for a more formidable manipulation of Tense-differences, there is sonnet 129 which is 'objective', but where the point of reference is surely the Dark Lady:

> Th'expence of Spirit in a waste of shame
> *Is* lust in action, and *till* action, lust
> *Is* perjurd, murdrous, blouddy full of blame,
> Savage, extreame, rude, cruell, not *to trust*,
> *Injoyed no sooner but dispised straight,*
> Past reason *hunted*, and *no sooner had*,
> Past reason *hated as a swollowed bayt*,
> On purpose *layd to make* the taker mad:
> Mad in pursut and in possession so,
> *Had, having,* and *in quest, to have* extreame,
> A blisse *in proofe* and prov'd, a very woe,
> *Before a joy proposed, behind* a dreame,
> All this the world well *knowes*, yet none *knowes* well,
> *To shun* the heaven that *leads* men to this hell.

My italics show the difficulties confronting us if we would attempt to demonstrate the extent of the contribution of the Verb in a passage of verse by Shakespeare where he is exploiting its formal inflexions. We are so used to the comparatively inactive consistencies of the Verb in nineteenth-century poetry, where effective variation of grammatical Tense and consequent inter-play between Tenses is a rare thing and where so much less *happens* (verbs betoken happenings) as a consequence. But in contemplating the verbs, in some passage of Shakespeare, where they are particularly numerous and alert, it is not sufficient to mark only those inflexions of those words to which grammarians would restrict the name of Verb. Not only the Participles but the Adverbs, particularly those of Time, when they modify the Verbs have to be taken into account.

The Verbal Dynamics of this sonnet on Lust articulate a recurrent experience: as it is in prospect (exciting, violent, blissful), and as it is in retrospect (shameful, horrible, wasteful, deceptive); lust as thus → and, the lust expended, thus ←, and between these temporal arrowheads is, to quote Tourneur's phrase, that "poor benefit of a bewildering minute",[1] yet not

---

[1] I follow the Mermaid text here. Allardyce Nicoll, in his edition of Tourneur, has "bewitching".

seen as 'poor' in advance of its 'hereness', or actuality, when the present Tense is operative.

Yet, it will be seen that, within the short space of a sonnet, the two arrowheads do not confront each other only once. They do so three times, though each statement of this Future-Past opposition is briefer than its predecessor, as its truth becomes increasingly known and asserted, while still leaving room for a concluding couplet.

Now, in *Macbeth*, lust is not the action, but, as in the sonnet just considered, the 'joy proposed' (possession of the Crown), becomes, when 'prov'd', 'a very woe'—the woe of disillusion, of expectancy cheated. And since it is a play whose Verbs are so clear and important, I shall turn to it next.

2 'MACBETH': TENSE AND MOOD

The Form of the Verb of *Macbeth*, that which controls the whole plot, is peculiarly striking. It is, of course, the Future Indicative. But the dominant form of the Verb 'in' *Macbeth*, that which animates not the main outlines but the detail of passages, is also significant. It is the Subjunctive. The Verb Form 'of' *Macbeth* and the Verb Form 'in' *Macbeth* struggle against each other, and from this struggle issues the tragedy. It is the struggle which creates the 'action', as distinguished from the mere 'plot', of *Macbeth*.

Since the Future Indicative is the Tense expressive of future *facts*—of events, things, conditions which *will be*, the main and auxiliary Verbs here equally stressed—it is the necessary Tense of a plot whose substance is a prophecy made to Macbeth "that shalt be King hereafter" (I. iii. 50), a prophecy later followed by other prophecies.

But the Witches, whose function it is to foretell, and who open the play with a question framed in that Tense ("When shall we three meet again?"), are not the only ones who use the Future Indicative. For Macbeth and Banquo, respectively, echo the Witches' words:

> Your Children shall be Kings.
> You shall be King.

> (I. iii. 86)

and, in so echoing, lean away from the Present they are in, each following his dread, the other's hope, into the Future. Next, Lady Macbeth, when told of the prophecy by letter, cries:

> Glamys thou art, and Cawdor, and shalt be
> What thou art promis'd.
>
> (I. v. 16)

Moreover, she not only wills the Future but she goes ahead out of her time into that Tense, experiencing its sensation, as she says to Macbeth:

> Thy Letters have transported me beyond
> This ignorant present, and I feele now
> The future in the instant.
>
> (I. v. 57)

Yet even those ignorant of the prophecy express themselves in the Future. If they do not look forward to coming certainties, they have intentions, and these acts of the will require for their expression this Tense. Thus Duncan:

> I have begun to plant thee, and will labour
> To make thee full of growing.
>
> (I. iv. 28)

> We will establish our Estate upon
> Our eldest, *Malcome* . . .
>
> (I. iv. 37)

> . . . signes of Noblenesse, like Starres, shall shine
> On all deservers.
>
> (I. iv. 41)

Indeed, the whole play is Future minded, thus →. Unlike *Hamlet* and *Othello* there are in it no temporal flashbacks, no protracted memories of earlier generations, no narrations of past events, but it purely and avidly pursues a Future, and that is why reader and audience derive from it a sensation of rapidity or hurrying.

But if the Future Indicative drives the play as a whole, there is also that other Verb Form which informs the detail of parts, first and particularly in the Speeches of Macbeth himself. Now the Subjunctive is started into life hard upon the Witches' statement of fact that Macbeth "shalt be King hereafter":

> Macbeth: . . . .
>   . . . Present Feares
> Are lesse than horrible Imaginings:
> My thought, whose Murther yet is but fantasticall,
> Shakes so my single state of Man,
> That Function is smother'd in surmise,
> And nothing is, but what is not.
>
> (I. iii. 137)

Here we are not in the indicative world of facts (of what is, has been, or will be) but in the subjunctive realm of *possibilities*— the realm of hopes and dreads; of 'if's' and phantasies; of what may be and may not be; of what ought to be and what ought not to be. The Subjunctive is a private realm and so Macbeth speaks 'aside', for though we may all have to share the world of fact (is-ness), yet each man's subjunctive realm is his alone. In the lines quoted, Macbeth moves over into that realm denoted, we remember by the *recto* pages, where the Verbs are conjugated, in Kennedy's *Latin Primer*. Now the Subjunctive can be the realm of "horrible Imaginings". The Future Indicative of the Witches precipitates Macbeth—as it does not Lady Macbeth who professes scorn for the Mood—into that realm, and habitation therein eventually destroys him. Not that it was perhaps necessary for him to inhabit it at all, as Macbeth himself suspects, since, after the Witches' statement of a simple future fact, he says:

> If Chance will have me King,
> Why Chance may Crowne me,
> Without my stirre.
>
> (I. iii. 143)

Yet the two verbs in these three lines belong to different grammatical Moods.

Now Lady Macbeth well knows her husband's disposition to move into the Subjunctive and so brake the wheels of indicative action. She says of him:

>   Thou would'st be great,
> Art not without Ambition, but without
> The illnesse should attend it. What thou would'st highly,
> That would'st thou holily: would'st not play false,

And yet would'st wrongly winne.
Thould'st have, great Glamys, that which cryes,
Thus thou must doe, if thou have it;
And that which rather thou do'st feare to doe,
Then wishest should be undone.

(I. v. 19)

Here two Indicatives stand out: Macbeth *is* ambitious; he *is* without that immunity from qualms of conscience which an ambitious man, to succeed in his ambitions, *ought* to have. Yet conscience, the umpire which distinguishes between moral 'ought's and 'ought-not's operates in the Subjunctive Mood—where its verdicts may well clash with desires which also belong to that Mood. So when Lady Macbeth says her husband *is* without the immunity from conscience which *should* (i.e. ought to) go with ambition she is being curiously casuistical: an ambitious man *ought* not to be concerned with 'ought's and 'ought-not's; Macbeth *ought*, in this case, to make the Future fact a Present fact through "the neerest way" of indicative action. But, in Macbeth's subjunctive realm, his wishes ("thou *would'st* be great . . . thou *would'st* highly . . . *would'st* wrongly winne") clash with moral duty ("That *would'st* thou holily: *would'st* not play false").

Until a deed is done it does not exist in time. Desires and duties timelessly exist in a world of "perpetual possibility",[1] have speculative actuality only, unless and until they are transferred, by a choice of the will resulting in action, on to those left-hand pages of Kennedy's conjugations. But Macbeth would have the *real* goods without experiencing the responsibility for their conversion from subjunctive desire to indicative fact; desires should 'materialize' of their own accord without the consent of his will and without his "stirre". Alternatively:

The Eye winke at the Hand; yet let that bee,
Which the Eye feares, when it is done to see.

(I. iv. 52)

'Let the deed be done without the consent of my will *or* let it be done without my knowing that I do it.' The disintegration of Macbeth's personality, to use the fashionable parlance of psychiatrists, concretely conveyed—as here—in terms of one

[1] T. S. Eliot, *Burnt Norton*.

51

sense (or organ) functioning in dissociation from another or others has been noticed.[1] But the grammatical structure of this condition should be borne in mind. The imagery means that Macbeth hopes that the *instrumental* organ of indicative action (his hand) should perform in isolation from the organ of perception which must 'winke' so that his conscience does not have to sanction the deed of his hand. He must both have his cake and eat it. He must translate subjunctive desire into indicative possession and yet keep himself pure and innocent within his subjunctive realm. This is supported by two other grammatical features. Instead of 'when I have done it . . . etc.', we find "yet let that bee,/ Which the Eye feares, *when it is done* to see".[2] By employing the Passive Voice, he escapes from having to say 'I'. He employs grammatical mechanisms whereby he is enabled to *distance* the murder from himself, to reduce or eschew responsibility for it (*it is done: I* don't do it), and to avoid giving the sin and crime its name. This is psychologically true: when people are in misery they can hardly bear to mumble 'I'—their 'I' lies low; when people are in moral or legal difficulties they try to shield themselves by using the Passive Voice.

The two main Verb Forms, the determining Future Indicative of the plot and the Subjunctive of Macbeth, which threatens to—illogically—prevent that which "shalt be", engage each other in the most strenuous conflict in the famous soliloquy of Macbeth in I. vii. 1–28. We should notice the intense and violent activity of the Verbs in this passage. Even numerically, compared with other Parts of Speech, they are of overwhelming importance. Few, if any, other passages of verse of similar length in English can compare with it in this respect. And these Verbs are significant and exciting because of the variety of their inflexional forms, involving contrasts of Tense, Mood and Voice, for Macbeth is contemplating not only alternative states of being; possibilities of action and inaction, of desire, deed and duty; but also Time, that time or tense which takes control once the transference from Mood to Mood is performed. He begins:

> If it were done, when 'tis done, then 'twere well
> It were done quickly; If th'Assassination

[1] See, for example, the introduction by Kenneth Muir to his Arden edition of the play.

[2] Italics, here and elsewhere, unless marked in the Folios, are mine.

Could trammell up the Consequence, and catch
With his surcease, Successe: that but this blow
Might be the be all, and the end all. Heere,
But heere, upon this Banke and Schoole of time,
Wee'ld jumpe the life to come. But in these Cases,
We still have judgement heere, that we but teach
Bloody Instructions, which being taught, returne
To plague th' Investor. . . .

(I. vii. 1)

The opening line and a half of the speech consists of a series
of Subjunctive Clauses. Since 'the deed', which is still merely
possible, for the will must choose before the hand strikes, is
being contemplated, each of the verbs in each of these clauses
is a variant of the one Verb *to do*, and all these clauses are
dependent on a speculative, and therefore subjunctively expressed, state of ease and goodness—" 'twere well", itself merely
contingent. Apart from the connectives and the temporal Adverb "quickly", the only non-verb component is the Subject
common to all the clauses. The Subject, if it were named,
would be 'the deed' which is to be done; but, still not daring
to name, he *pro*-names: the Pronoun 'it' is a generalizing substitute for something unmentionable. Further, the series of
Verbs of which it is the subject are all in the *Passive* Subjunctive:
Macbeth will still distance the possible 'thing' from himself and
conceal from himself his own *active* agency, pretending that the
deed did not require a do-er.

Also there are the curious temporal implications of these and
the following lines. In a play which, from the premises of its
plot, is Future-driven, Macbeth, especially, is one who cannot
be in his Present. Though Lady Macbeth "feeles the future in
the instant", she does not do so as Macbeth does. He projects
himself not only into the Future Indicative (Lady Macbeth,
believing the prophecy, does this), but also into the possible, the
Future Subjunctive, as the soliloquy shows. In this, like all born
worriers, he apprehends a Future deed from a future still more
remote. He "ore-leapes". Assuming a possible deed done (so
that it has entered the time-stream and become Past action)
then results *will* be certain: Duncan's Vertues "*will* pleade like
Angels" and "teares *shall* drowne the winde". So he chooses not
to do. But he is overborne by Lady Macbeth, and the real and

53

the potential fuse at the moment that Duncan's heart ceases to beat.

Now it would be to miss something, significant and in itself beautiful, if one did not also note the one considerable respite from *Macbeth's* ruling Verb Forms in favour of the Present.

Act I, sc. vi has long been praised as 'charming' and 'idyllic', etc. But has it been observed that it owes much of its peacefulness to the fact that Duncan salutes the Castle in the grace, the felicity of his Present?

> This Castle hath a pleasant seat,
> The ayre nimbly and sweetly recommends it selfe
> Unto our gentle sences.

Thus innocents enjoy themselves—in their own good time. Indeed, this contentment in the moment with what the moment brings extends to Banquo in the same scene:

> This Guest of Summer,
> The Temple-haunting Martlet does approve,
> By his loved Mansionry, that the Heavens breath
> Smells wooingly here. . . .

The 'martlets' *are showing* their approval and the air is *being* noticed as fragrant. The sense of relaxation which this scene creates is surely as much owing to the Tense, suspending here the play's furious future-drive, as to the lines' soothing melody or delightful imagery.

In Act III, sc. i King Macbeth finds that:

> To be thus, is nothing, but to be safely thus.

Shakespeare is again using three contrasting Forms of one and the same Verb—*to be*. Now, *to be* is a simple Verb: simple in the sense that its conjugation is given primary attention in any elementary Grammar of any language. Yet that whole soliloquy of Macbeth (in III. i), which this line initiates, is an essay in the semantics of the two primary Verbs *to be* and *to have*, on a Present-Future Tense axis. For Macbeth is (King) but is not (King) securely. He *has* a 'Crowne' but it *will be* 'fruitlesse'; he has a 'Scepter' but it *is* barren and it *will be* 'wrencht' away. Macbeth is still at once both chasing and fearing that Future, fixed in the words with which he re-stated the Witches' prophecy, to Banquo: "Your Children shall be Kings". Having arrived at his goal, Macbeth finds that the goal has moved on further into the Future. 'Thou shall get Kings, though thou be none' (I. iii), the Witches had told Banquo. But that prophecy was in *Indicative* terms, and so cannot be prevented. This Macbeth should know when he summons 'Fate into the Lyst'. As a worrier, he is still knocking about in times other than his own, but now in a different kind of time than in I. vii, partly because what was then possible and Subjunctive has *been* enacted, has come into the order of time and is now Past. Moreover, since the Subjunctive counsel of 'ought's' and 'ought-not's' was neglected, when Macbeth murdered Duncan, this Mood no longer exists for him. Macbeth is, as he tells us, damned. Damnation is a state where the Subjunctive does not exist. So, from Act III, sc. i onwards, the Present-Future time-swaying is different, and vainer. Macbeth would, but cannot, prevent a prophecy. His own time-scale of living has altered so much that the only policy left is 'hurry and try to overtake'— a sort of vain pursuit, half-known to be vain. He will lean forwards into time to try to snip, at some point, the linked navel cords leading from Banquo to a Future Indicative King of Scotland. But he is made to know final failure when the Witches show him the seed of Banquo, stretching—as Kings— "out to th' Cracke of Doome" (IV. i). Yet he will still try.

So from this Act III, sc. i the Poetic-Dramatic Grammar of Time changes rapidly in *Macbeth*. It is a case of the Past catching up with him in league with a Future foreclosing upon him, as the detailed rendering of Tense in the verse shows. Chased by the Past, he *will* attempt to move more quickly than the Future, as in:

> Time, thou anticipat'st my dread exploits:
> The flighty purpose never is o're-tooke
> Unless the deed go with it. From this moment,
> The very firstlings of my heart shall be
> The firstlings of my hand. And even now
> To Crown my thoughts with Acts: be it thought and done:
> The Castle of Macduff, I will surprise.
>
> (IV. i. 144)

But he cannot succeed, and meanwhile the *overtaking* forces have gathered and pursue.

The Play-Tense and Mood of *Macbeth*, considered as a whole, is that of → or Future/. The → represents the drive from a discounted Present. It is not only Macbeth and Lady Macbeth who discount the Present. Duncan also, as we have seen, is full of 'intentions'. Banquo, to whom has been said "your Children shall be Kings", is also forward-looking. So is the orphaned Malcolm. So is the widowed and childless man, Macduff. He has a revenge to undertake and a revenge is a future-looking action; for a *revenger* is certainly one who discounts the Present in the expectancy of an end or satisfaction. Finally, and they are the most important in serving the →, in terms of the plot which they thrust, are the Witches, who are 'Jugling Fiends'

> That keepe the word of promise to our eare,
> And breake it to our hope.
>
> (V. viii. 21)

Which leads us to the bar: / in our formula. The explanation of the bar lies in the two lines just quoted. It is the bar / which makes this play, and much in life, tragic. The Witches prophesy and promise, and Macbeth leans forward in mind to greet in hope more than they verily promise. Macbeth, in hoping for more than is promised, security of tenure and succession by his own line, is irrational; but then hope, from its definition and nature, is irrational.

The hope is broken, not so much because the 'Jugling Fiends' 'palter . . . in a double sence', but because they are literal-minded, utter only the literal truth, give literal prophecies which are indicatively fulfilled. The wood of Birnam *does* come to Dunsinane. Before that, Macbeth *has* become King and, in the future, Banquo's descendants *will* become Kings. The tragedy issued from Macbeth for believing in more than the literal.

The 'more' he believed in, Shakespeare says, was the 'more' of hope. Hope is not the 'will be' of the Indicative, but a 'may be', or a 'might be', sustained in faith until a target-date is reached, or protracted even beyond that, depending on the temper of him who hopes. If the hope is broken in time—elapse of time is needed for defeat, as for fulfilment of hope—then it becomes a 'might have been'. The Grammatical Mood for the spiritual condition of hope is therefore the Subjunctive. The bar in our Tense formula for *Macbeth* is the simple block of the Indicative fact: namely, Banquo's children 'will be Kings'. Macbeth, witnessing the show put on for him of the crowned seed of Banquo stretching out in temporal recession to the 'Cracke of Doome', sees what indicatively *will be* as an *is*. That is the extreme torment, but the play is a tragedy. The Subjunctive of hope in Macbeth can never become 'realized' or Indicative. The cheque always turns out to be post-dated.

After the banquet scene he is "bent to know/ By the worst meanes the worst" (III. iv. 134), but the new knowledge culminated in that "horrible sight" of Banquo's descendants stretching out into a Futurity only limited by doomsday. Yet Macbeth will still try to circumvent the certain facts of a Future although the attempt must necessarily fail. This is paradoxical but so it is. The results also involve a temporal paradox best appreciated at a stage-performance: Birnam wood marches against him at Dunsinane where Macbeth is overtaken by the Future, before he can pre-vent it.

What creates the peculiar → Future /, or Arrow to Future Bar, Play-Tense of *Macbeth*? And by Play-Tense we mean, as we hope will now be apparent, something other than either the time the work takes to act or read, or some time-table of events (e.g. 'Act II takes place in the early hours of the following day') on the pattern of P. A. Daniel. All the elements combine to create it, but we especially point to (1) elements in the verse itself, particularly the exceptional frequency of occurrence of the Future Indicative and (ii) the plot, or dramatic aspect, which rests on prophecy. Yet verse and plot are not really separable at all. For instance, the line 'All haile Macbeth, that *shalt be* King hereafter' is clearly an example of both (i) and (ii), and the 'hereafter' indicates that temporal qualification, capable of infinite postponement, which signalizes that /, or bar, of the tragedy.

3 PLAY-TENSES: EARLY AND MIDDLE PERIODS

In the *Sonnets* we saw that Shakespeare's choice between 'thou' and 'you' in any one context depended, among other things, on his awareness or otherwise of the one he loved as subject to Time, that is mortal; and that the Verb inflexions, governed by one or the other Pronoun, similarly register the absence or presence of this awareness. Now, we could relate what we have found of the behaviour of Pronouns and Verb forms in Shakespeare's *Sonnets* to his plays. But that is altogether too ambitious for a book of this kind, and since I have already considered *Macbeth* in some detail, the remarks which follow on other plays must perforce be much more general and the stress will be on what I have called—in the *Macbeth* section—the *Play-Tenses* rather than on the particular Verb inflexions *within* the plays, while Pronouns will receive more cursory notice still. All that is offered is an initiatory attempt which should invite later refinement or a breaking down into severer categories.

The Romantic Comedies

The Tense and Mood of the Romantic Comedies is, like the Tense of the 'thou'-sonnets, a Continuous Present resistant to change—this in spite of such objections as that the march of the seasons is forcibly noticed in *Love's Labour's Lost*; that a few nocturnal hours wreak reversals of fortune in *A Midsummer Night's Dream*; that expiry in time of a legal bond is essential to the plot of *The Merchant of Venice*; or that the relativity of time is much disputed in *As You Like It*, Act III, sc. ii. All that is true: time passing is of vital importance in the conduct, to the credibility, and to the manipulation of plot in these comedies, but it is still time *of a kind*, which passes.

By 'of a kind' I mean that it is of the same kind as the time which passes in the early 'thou'-sonnets. It is the kind necessary for a stance and an argument in the Sonnets, and it is the kind necessary for a *plot*, any kind of plot, in a play. A dramatist, almost any dramatist of almost any period, must assume the passage of time as a convention needed for the unity of his play. This convention is just of the order we encounter on the programme of a West End play today, e.g. 'Act I: scene—Sir Arthur X's study; it is in the morning. Act II—the same on the evening of the same day; Act III—Sir Arthur's living-room—three years afterwards.' From this it will be seen that we are not concerned directly, however much it may be indirectly involved, with what is known as the Elizabethan stage's 'continuity of action'.[1]

Irrespective of their various plot-times, the real and sustaining Tense of the Romantic Comedies is the same as that of the early *Sonnets*, a Continuous Present, however much another, and perhaps more interesting, order of Time might be implicit and be detected to gradually emerge as Shakespeare, through the passage of years, came to have a lengthening past and a narrowing future, and put his experience of this to use. By Continuous Present we designate a Tense where Past, Present and Future of the plot all move *against* the sense of a continuous *Now*, and I hope this sense is something Professor G. Wilson Knight would recognize as part of the 'atmosphere' or 'spatial designs' of these comedies. Now, the Continuous Present of these plays is the Tense that all youth, at any period of history, most naturally *lives* or inhabits, though the memory of being there may be hard to stir once those physiological changes have taken place within us, changes which alter our personality and endue us with another and altogether more harassing sense of Time.

Shakespeare's rate of development between 1594 and 1598 was much reduced as a result of the early deaths of Greene, Marlowe and Kyd, whose continued rivalry would have stimulated his own growth. Up to 1598, when the new and original force of Jonson begins to be reflected in the work of Shakespeare, we see only a gradual fading of that Continuous Present. But after 1598, though it may intermittently or momentarily revive as echo or memory, it becomes supplanted by that order of Tenses whose system is organized on the principle of the flux of Time, as is seen in the 'you'-sonnets (e.g. "When I consider every thing that growes/Holds in perfection but a little moment", 15), and which is based on a felt observation of mortality. His body came to inform Shakespeare that it must endure dissolution, and he increasingly came to communicate this knowledge to certain of his *dramatis personae*, through the

[1] Yet a general acknowledgment for what follows is due to the late S. L. Bethell's *Shakespeare and the Popular Dramatic Tradition*.

handling of Tense in his poetry. Previously to this, deaths—
though many had seemed to occur in, say, the early Histories
or in *Titus Andronicus*—had not been really believed in, or
genuinely felt, by the author. Nor are they felt by any modern
audience.

The beauty and achievement of the early plays, including
Romeo and Juliet, have to be relished within a conventional
acceptance of the Continuous Present. They move in time
before us—'two howres traffique' showing the events of a few
days and nights—and yet are still. Consider *The Merchant of
Venice*. Although we accept that the plot-motive is the expiry of
a date on a legal bond resulting in penalties, are we—or is
Shakespeare—more advanced in Time when at length we
arrive at Belmont in Act V, sc. i, and hear the speeches beginning "The moon shines bright . . .", or "How sweet the
moon-light sleepes upon this banke"? As a matter of fact, all the
verbs in the entire speech of Lorenzo, from which the latter
quotation comes, are in the Present Indicative, and the whole
scene up to, and beyond, this point, creates the sense that "such
a night as this", which Lorenzo and Jessica are enjoying, is
Continuously Present and is one with the night of all previous
lovers. The customary means for creating this Tense are the
inflexions of the ordinary Present Indicative vibrantly inter-
mingled with those of a tender Subjunctive of desire.

Indeed, if we look at the Romantic Comedies, we find this:
Except when the express business of plot machination required
such Futures as 'To-morrow, then, at the hour of noon we meet'
(invented to stand as an example of a hundred such hints), or
such I. i or I. ii plot-needed, expository, Pasts as 'My father
when he lived . . .' (likewise invented); except such cases, the
prevailing Tense throughout is the Present Indicative. Against
this Prevailing Tense frequently sound—to give the effect of
bitter-sweetness, of lyrical pathos—the notes of a Subjunctive
of desire, an 'O, that I serv'd that Lady' sort of thing, which
eventually cease at the end of a play where desire is satisfied and
all ends well. Yet all this happens outside or beyond the
dimension of actual Time, ageing and tissue-destroying Time.
There is no clock in the forest of Arden, in the palace of Illyria,
or in the grounds of Belmont. These plays exist outside Time.
Why is this so? Is it not because it is only on the assumption of a

Continuous Present that original desires can be satisfied—without their renunciation, diversion, or modification in the *process* of striving towards them?

The Early Histories

In the early Histories the need, on the part of Shakespeare, to follow a rigorous sequence of actual events, as recorded in Hall or Holinshed, enforced itself. But the time of these plays is 'chronicle time', and chronicle time is not far removed from the time of the historical pageant. The characters speak at the end in the same mode as they spoke at the beginning—without benefit of experience. Their speech is the notation for a series of physical events beheld, or executed, by the *dramatis personae* without an alteration of the structure of their sensibilities. Yet a judgment of this kind is relative, for there are passages and hints, notably in *Richard II*, for example, which anticipate the apprehension of the Time of the 'you'-sonnets or of *Troilus*. Thus it was through the 'chronicle time' of the Histories, rather than through the Continuous Present of the Comedies, that Shakespeare slowly developed his knowledge of Time: a knowledge which was to later result in the masterful manipulations of Tense in later plays. This was so because of their subject-matter. The word 'history', for Hall and Holinshed, implied above all a record of events in time in the order in which they occurred. With the chronicles (in place of those *novelle* whose time is Romance-Time) before him, Shakespeare was forced to use the Past and Future tenses in frequent relation to the Present, even though what he narrates or shows is largely the sequence of merely physical events. Yet however more enterprising in Tense-range, the Histories are more restricted in grammatical and poetic *Mood* than the Comedies. The composition of the early Histories involved a steady and persistent exercise in the use of Past, Present and Future Indicative inflexions. In showing what is and was and, occasionally, what *will* be instead of what is *desired*, the Subjunctive Mood was seldom called on. Yet, as a measure of what Shakespeare attained, with respect to poetic flexibility and force, through the packing of contrasting Tenses—that is, of varying Time-perspectives—within a single passage of verse, reference should be made to *Richard II*, Act III, sc. ii. In the speech of the

King beginning: "No matter where, of comfort no man speake", much of the melancholy and powerful resonance must be attributed to a series of clauses whose Verbs are in contrasting Tenses. What Richard says is now near in time, now remote, now in the temporal "middle-distance"; now the near (and menacing) future foreshadows itself, next the pitiful present has its voice. Here is poetry that commingles continually-varying Time-perspectives, and thereby contrasting emotions are also commingled.

Henry IV, Part I and Part II

But it is in *Henry IV*, especially in Part II, that we really find the kind of awareness that informs the 'you'-sonnets, such sonnets as nos. 63, 65, 67, 68,[1] where Shakespeare came to know himself as a slow-dying subject of Time; the young man in his 'you-ness', a creature of body and soul, to be also mortal, and his love for him contingent on circumstance; the Continuous Present of the 'thou'-sonnets, in which his love and his poetry are immortal, to be not so much untrue as incomplete, possibly even to be belied by later reflection and by what we call experience—a load of memories acting on one another.

In *Henry IV*, the poetic-dramatic Tense is not the 'chronological time' Tense of the early Histories. It is true that, as in the early Histories, a vague and indeterminate number of years are 'covered' in accord with the source. Henry actually reigned for thirteen years but the period seems much longer in the plays because of the weight of back-reference. But this source which supplied the chronological time is overborne by a sense of other forces. These forces cannot have precise names given them but can only be alluded to in such terms as the following: Memory, experience, accumulation, pastness, the process of decay. In *Henry IV*, especially in Part II, more so than any previous play, Shakespeare is concerned with a Past Indicative, a past where seemingly irredeemable sins were committed, a past whose banefulness is still acting on its consequence, the present. In the text itself, Past forms of the Verbs come to have a great say, the more remarkable when one remembers that the normal Verb Tense in any drama is the

[1] L. C. Knights has done much to aid our understanding of the relation of *Henry IV* to certain of the sonnets.

Present, just as the normal Tense of narrative verse is the Past. Yet no wonder that this is so, especially since so many 'characters' on so many occasions throughout this double-play remember the past in relation to the present or blame it for the miserable and, by contrast, inadequate present. They try, as though they were judges, their own actions and those of others in the past. They consciously consider what 'is' to issue from what 'was'. The 'present' King, and the 'present' rebels recall each his, or their, service to the other in the past, and charge the other with ingratitude—an emotion which, of its nature, always balances past against present. They remember the past King and what he said ("Northumberland, thou ladder . . .") and realize what was prophesied then has become only too true now.

But if the government and the rebels are chained to the past, surely Falstaff, to be the lord of life that he is, lives in the present? Initially that may be the case, though even then we are insistently reminded of his age and white hairs by Hall. But as the work goes on, his growing past and his shortening future weigh heavily on him, on the play, on us.

In no work, save perhaps in *Hamlet*, is Shakespeare so aware of process, or so aware of a corrupt present being— beyond choice—the issue of a corrupt, and still corrupting, past. The axis of Play-Tenses, on which *Henry IV* revolves, is Past-Present-Past. Gone now is the Romance innocence of the Continuous Present; gone too is Chronicle Time conceived of in terms of merely outward change.

At the very end of Part II there is indeed a jerk away from retrospective tense, where Prince John says:

> I will lay oddes, that ere this yeere expire,
> We beare our Civill Swords, and Native fire
> As farre as France. I heard a Bird so sing,
> Whose Musicke (to my thinking) pleas'd the King.
> (Part II, V. v. 111)

And certainly the Tense of *Henry V* is that of a short-sighted plain Future—a grasping at immediate ends through *physical* action, and a satisfaction from the exertion. But this play's invigorating coarseness, its lack of temporal perspectives, its by-and-large forgetfulness, its rejection of experience, should not blind us to the fact that in its predecessor Shakespeare attained a massiveness of utterance. This massiveness can be a great deal attributed to the *say* and *gainsay* of Past-Present-Past Indicatives in the detail of the verse, the tenses overlaying their meanings in a single passage of verse; can be attributed, more generally, to the oscillation of Past-Present-Past, when it is dramatically rendered in those scenes where 'King' and 'rebels' successively invoke the past as a comment on their present state; and can be attributed to the tone of the whole. In *Henry IV* Tense—and so Time—is no longer merely necessary for the mechanics of the plot to be set within a Continuous Present: on the contrary, it has become the poetic and dramatic substance, where the Subjunctive does not exist, is not believed in. Shakespeare is thus in the right condition for *Troilus and Cressida* or for *Measure for Measure*. In the latter the clash is between the Subjunctive of what man 'ought to do' and the Indicative of what he 'does'—and 'will do'—as Professor G. Wilson Knight showed so well in an essay in *The Wheel of Fire*. In this play there occurs a realistic defeat of the Gospel counsels of perfection, of what it *behoves* man to do.

Troilus and Cressida

As for *Troilus and Cressida*: the poetic-dramatic Tenses of this play (which, as most critics agree, is primarily concerned with the corrosive effects of that 'great siz'd monster of ingratitudes', Time, on the Subjunctive values) are supremely interesting.

Though, as in *Henry IV*, there is an apparent axis of strain between Present and Past, the Past perspective is not more remote than the few years during which the intolerably inconclusive siege has been going on. The active memory of the play does not stretch back further than the capture of Helen by Paris some nine years ago, and when Ulysses, speaking to Achilles of the current acts of valour by rival warriors, says:

> . . . Then what they doe in present,
> Though lesse then yours in past, must ore-top yours:
> For time is like a fashionable Hoste,
> That slightly shakes his parting Guest by th'hand;
> And with his armes out-stretcht, as he would flye,
> Graspes in the commer: the welcome ever smiles,

And farewell goes out sighing: O let not vertue seeke
Remuneration for the thing it was. . . .

(III. iii. 163)

it is the callous shortness of memory that is being insisted on.
The forgotten deeds of Achilles are those he wrought before he
but recently went into the sulks. Not only Cressida's but everyone else's memory is short, and we can be sure that the reason
is not because Shakespeare believed, as did Socrates, in the
Timaeus, that the Greeks, unlike the Egyptians, had a poor
sense of history.

We can contrast this harshly-limited memory of *Troilus* with
the memory of *Henry IV* which reaches back a generation, and
where the conscience, burdened with a recollection of sin, an
"impostume of corruption", makes the reign of Richard II
seem variously a 'yesterday' and an unreckonable age past
merging into the 'revolution of the Times' that, stretching
before and after,

> Make Mountaines levell, and the Continent
> (Wearie of solide firmenesse) melt it selfe
> Into the Sea . . .

(2 *Henry IV*, III. i. 47)

In *Troilus*, on the other hand, Time is callous because
memory is so short, and the Past is just behind, in the "abject
rear" of those now jostling forward. "Injurious time", we are
told, has "a robbers haste". Moreover, when Troilus sees
Cressida in Diomed's arms he does not say: "this is, but *was* not
Cressid", but: "this is, and is not Cressid" (V. ii). He says so
because this play's past treads so closely on the heels of the
present. It is from such key phrases that we learn that the Tense
of this play is not the Past-Present-Past, with a slow and large
pendulum swing, as in *Henry IV*, but that it is Present-Past-
Present, with a fast-swinging pendulum that describes but brief
arcs. But, though the play, in its temporal oscillation, involves
constant references to a meanly-limited past, the dominant
Verb inflexions in the verse of the play are those of the Present
Indicative, here a gritty Tense bespeaking harsh actuality. For
"it *is*, and *is* not Cressid", because

> Time hath, (my Lord) a wallet at his backe,
> Wherein he puts alms for oblivion:

65

A great-siz'd monster of ingratitudes:
These scraps are good deedes past,
Which are devour'd as fast as they are made,
Forgot as soone as done.

(III. iii. 145)

Yet is it not, at first thought, strange that the memory of *Troilus* should be so short? At the height of the so-called Renaissance, and with a plentitude of sources beside Chaucer, what subject might have seemed fitter for grand perspectives? A play founded on a subject to do with the siege could embrace within its memory the rise of the house of Atreus; Achilles' divine birth; the sacrifice of Iphigenia; particular campaigns over a space of ten years, and could similarly foresee (with a conviction and importance beyond that accorded to Cassandra's brief, frantic and vague interruption in I. iii) the fall of Troy; the death of Agamemnon; the founding of Rome; and even the settlement of Britain. No other material could have offered wider temporal span when dramatized, yet no other play of Shakespeare has such a restricted pendulum-swing, despite the fact that in it Time becomes a character himself, enacting the Present-Past-Present, and cramming "his rich theeverie up".

The explanation of this is that on one level at least, *Troilus and Cressida* is a Satire. Now Satire, on the basis of its first assumptions, its reference to what the audience recognizes as topical, requires the Present Tense as its instrument. A writer does not satirize figures of the past and the Rome of Jonson's *Poetaster* is recognizably London at the time Jonson wrote it; and his audience knew that Horace was Jonson in disguise. Hence the Verbs are in the Present Indicative, whether in *The Poetaster* or *Volpone*, unless a scheme—as part of the plot mechanics—is being unfolded to take effect on the morrow. (However Jonson, in observing the Unities, tends to have no to-morrow.) In the art of Satire a moment is isolated. The satiric attitude cannot survive in conjunction with a comprehension of the past: the past is too majestic, too full of waste and suffering, too demanding of respect or pity; if invoked, then the artificially isolated moment becomes lost.

Troilus and Cressida is not all—or only—Satire, but it has been persuasively suggested that it is Shakespeare's contribution to the 'War of the Theatres' and that the characters are contemporary personages in disguise.[1] Ulysses may be Francis Bacon even. Be that as it may, in *Troilus* Shakespeare may well be reacting to the force and example of the dramatist Jonson and this would explain the compression of the temporal scale of his play. We are shown a hard actuality, an is-ness, not contrasted with a magnificent past—nor with the Gospel or with a Romance system of ideal subjunctives—but in isolation.

In Sonnet 106, we have the lines:

> When in the Chronicle of wasted time,
> I see descriptions of the fairest wights,
> And beautie making beautifull old rime,
> In praise of Ladies dead, and lovely Knights . . .

But a sense of that Continuous Present is now—at least for the time being—dead in Shakespeare. In *Troilus and Cressida*, despite its Ladies and lovely Knights, not only the Tense of these lines, but also what we must call their content, only live and mean something—paradoxically—by their absence.

4   THE FINAL PLAYS: TRANSLATION OF MOOD

Since I do not pretend to offer a study, still less an exhaustive one, of the Verb Forms and Play-Tenses of the whole of Shakespeare but simply suggest lines of approach for such a study, merely developing enquiry in the case of a few particular plays such as *Macbeth*, I shall next turn to the Final Plays. This is to neglect the rich possibilities offered by a discussion of some of the other tragedies. In a book of this scope that cannot be avoided. All one can do here is to note that in none of the others is the Future thrust so evident and unimpeded as in *Macbeth*.

In *Hamlet*, for example, the slowness of the tempo is kept regulated by continual references to the past. Hamlet is set a task of revenge. This is a future-looking action, but its execution is retarded by Hamlet's habit of "looking before and after"; his memory behaves as a clog. Moreover, Polonius reminisces and Claudius, unlike Macbeth, is remorseful. Only Fortinbras is purely forward-looking, but he is too small a component to counter-balance scales so loaded with memories of deeds and persons anterior to the business shown on the stage.

[1] See O. J. Campbell, *Comicall Satyre and Shakespeare's Troilus and Cressida*.

In *Othello*, despite occasional flashbacks, as when Othello admits that he had told Desdemona his life-story (and so re-tells it to the Venetian Senate), or as when he tells Desdemona the history of the handkerchief he had given her—in both cases the past is given contemporary urgency—the inflexions belong to the present or immediate future. Time barely keeps up with stage-events. Deeds are hastily carried out without an adequate testing of motive, without a consideration of method and before their moral or even practical results are calculated. Hence the Verbs are hard put to it to keep up with such impulsiveness. An intention is scarcely promulgated before we find it is done: hence the Future inflexions have but brief validity; rapidly undergoing mutation they surrender themselves to a devouring Present. At the conclusion one can scarcely believe that the deed is done and the tragedy irreversible. One's mind, scarcely bent to its possibility, is overtaken by the act itself.

Finally, however much one hesitates to apply a shorthand note to a play so incredibly vast, there is *Lear*. Its present is expansive. In this tragedy each minute of suffering becomes, as it were, an aeon, for the measure here is not the clock but the breath drawn in pain. Only when the breaths are no longer drawn can Time contract to its accustomed proportions.

But to turn to the subject of this section. The huge temporal scope of the Final Play, and the consequent verbial[1] complexity of their detail, is the correlative of their Tense design. The control of such a design demanded less a direct passionate engagement in experience—erotic and mortual—than a memory of such, a detachment.

It has been suggested, by Professor William Empson, of the Final Plays, that Shakespeare cheats by bringing in a second generation. The point being, I suppose, that characters in the plays create for themselves a tragic problem beyond Shakespeare's power to solve on their own behalf, and that he gets out of the difficulty by bringing in others to solve it for them. This is not quite fair, for though the active importance

---

[1] 'Verbial', of or pertaining to the verb, does not appear in the *Shorter Oxford Dictionary*. But an adjective, readily distinguishable from the general 'verbal', is required.

of the children in these plays becomes acute at the point when they become nubile, they are significant before this in that they remind the parents of their own childhood.

These plays are a testimony of a revived belief in the Subjunctive. Trust of this Mood, whether expressive of desire or duty, had diminished with the retreat of the Continuous Present and the realization of 'you' in the *Sonnets*; since the demonstration of a cause and effect determinism in *Henry IV*; since the emergence of the brute actuality of the Indicative in *Troilus*; and since the defeat of hopes, and of what *ought to be*, in the Tragedies. But now, in these plays, Shakespeare is going to create a belief in it. Yet to create his belief in the Subjunctive it is necessary to translate from that Mood into the Indicative. Only if the desired does become actual is it worthy of belief. Thomas Didymus deserves respect, perhaps devotion, in that only he received a particular satisfaction. He had a brave mind, an impatient tongue, and saw to it that he would not be cheated.

I shall take *The Winter's Tale* as representative of the whole movement of soul. The memory of this play, if we compare it with *Henry IV* or certain sonnets—whose memory embraces geological time—is certainly not long, extending only as far back as the childhood of Polixenes and Leontes. But that childhood is far away in the past, it belongs to the lost golden age. It is so remote because it is so lost. Of that time, which they shared together, Polixenes says:

> We were as twyn'd Lambs, that did frisk i'th'Sun,
> And bleat the one at th'other: what we chang'd,
> Was Innocence, for Innocence: we knew not
> The Doctrine of ill-doing, nor dream'd
> That any did: Had we pursu'd that life,
> And our weake Spirits ne're been higher rear'd
> With stronger blood, we should have answer'd Heaven
> Boldly, not guilty; the Imposition clear'd,
> Hereditarie ours.
>
> (I. ii. 67)

In this statement of the extent of the backward look, the Verbs, for four and a half lines, are in the Past Perfect. What happened is now safely locked away, and now time and experience intervene between the speaker and what he reports as lost. That it is lost is expressed by the Pluperfect Subjunctive of Condition which follows: "Had we pursued . . ." This tense, beyond all others, expresses hopelessness; bespeaking gone chances or choices. It is a Tense which craves pity or indulgence of those to whom it is addressed; it is used to justify resentfulness or excuse indolence. "Had we pursued . . .", says Polixenes. But they did not pursue, and so can only *remember* a past stage of innocence, presently exemplified by Mamilius; and, while enduring their present condition of 'mature dignities' (I. i), realize their original condition has changed for a worse. Here, then, is an instance, early in the play, of a layering of Tense and Mood. But the overlaying of contrasting Temporal (Past-Present) states by Modal (might have been—was—might yet be) variations, as seen in this particular speech, is characteristic of *The Winter's Tale*, and of the other Final Plays, as structural wholes.

If the effective past of *The Winter's Tale* is restricted to, and contained within, the memory of two Kings in the middle way of their mortal life, the forward reach has by Time's hourglass much the same span. That personage says:

> Impute it not a crime
> To me, or my swift passage, that I slide
> Ore sixteene yeeres, and leave the growth untride
> Of that wide gap, since it is in my powre
> To orethrow Law, and in one selfe-borne howre
> To plant, and ore-whelme Custome.
>
> (IV. i. 4)

Though the "wide gap" is "untride" dramatically, we are given it narratively. In those terms Perdita has "growne in grace Equall with wondring" (IV. i), while for Leontes these same years have been slow in that state of grief where nothing seems to move without, for no movement occurs within. But neither steady "growth in grace", nor steady atonement, are critical. Neither Perdita nor Leontes therefore have had to choose, and so neither of them during the interval, which Time the Chorus bridges, are—as human figures—dramatic. Instead, both wait and slowly ripen towards a crisis which happening to one must happen to the other.

But before that there is the famous Sheep-Shearing festival of IV. iv. Until the rough question is put by the disguised Polixenes: 'Soft Swaine a-while, beseech you; Have you a Father?', this scene deserves, as we know, the adjectives that are conventionally bestowed on it: it is blissful, idyllic, jolly, enchanting, as commentators say. And that it also has great significance as well as charm has been shown in masterly fashion by G. Wilson Knight.[1] Yet the contribution of the Verb Forms to the peculiar quality of this scene should not be overlooked. From the opening:

> These your unusuall weeds, to each part of you
> Do's give a life: no Shepherdesse, but *Flora*
> Peering in Aprils front. This your sheepe-shearing,
> Is as a meeting of the petty Gods,
> And you the Queene on't,

to the disrupting question put by Polixenes to Florizel the dominant Form of Verb (except where the Old Shepherd recollects his deceased wife's behaviour on festal occasions) is an Intensive Present. This may be thought the usual Verb Form for those in love, while they are in each other's company, and so appropriate to this scene. But beyond its local contribution, it contributes—through an addition of a new temporal dimension—to the whole. One of its functions, for example, is that it recalls the passage in I. ii, where we were told that Polixenes and Leontes had experienced a pre-lapsarian innocence. Now we see the second generation re-enacting the state of their parents before they chose their fall. Here is an overlayering of which we—the audience or readers—are conscious but of which Perdita and Florizel are unconscious.

They are indeed unconscious that they are repeating any ancestral pattern, and we call the verb used the Present Intensive because, for them, it is the only Verb Form that does exist, and for Florizel there is no before or after. Each of Perdita's actions is a fulfilment of Florizel's wishes:

> What you do,
> Still betters what is done. When you speake (Sweet)
> I'ld have you do it ever: When you sing,
> I'ld have you buy, and sell so: so give Almes,

---

[1] In *The Crown of Life*, chapter III.

Pray so: and for the ord'ring your Affayres,
To sing them too. When you do dance, I wish you
A wave o'th Sea, that you might ever do
Nothing but that: move still, still so:
And owne no other Function. Each your doing,
(So singular, in each particular)
Crownes what you are doing, in the present deeds,
That all your Actes, are Queenes.

(IV. iv. 135)

But it cannot be said that this Intensive Present is identical with the Continuous Present of *The Merchant of Venice*, V. i (see above, p. 60). There Lorenzo and Jessica fancied themselves, likening themselves to pairs of lovers in the history of romance; here, the lovers are less sophisticated; unaware of Castiglione or Plato, they know only their own moment as real.[1]

Now, one may say that Florizel reveals that he is at 'the phase of infatuation', the pre-disillusion phase, or that he possesses the moment of maximum insight (note, incidentally, that Perdita is addressed as 'you'), according to one's temperament and later experience. That is not the point. The point is that at this phase of the play there is an apparent suspension of that time process which elsewhere disturbs and obsesses. Exempt from a concern for Past and Future, Florizel and Perdita live their moment—their Intensive Present—until Polixenes' question creates for them simultaneously a Past for which they are responsible and a Future for which they must act.

The Verb-Forms of the last scene, V. iii, are extraordinarily complex and subtle. Such they need to be, for though the scene consists of only one hundred and fifty-five lines, much has to be covered in retrospect as well as much enacted. Whether what is done is done fairly or is carried off by a *trompe d'œil* will, perhaps, always be disputed.

Of these few lines, the first twenty—up to the Stage Direction "Paulina draws a curtain and discovers Hermione standing as a statue"—summarily relate and re-enact the events of sixteen years.

Detailed examination reveals that the recollection, which is

[1] But, remembering Florizel's speech about " 'The gods themselves humbling their deities to love' ", what I have said must not be driven too far.

a re-enactment, of the experience of sixteen years—the time from which it all began up to the *now* of the stage direction—is conveyed by a series of tensal inflexions of the primary Verbs: to have, to be, to do:

> *Leontes:* O grave and good Paulina, the great comfort
> That I have had of thee?
> *Paulina:* What (Soveraigne Sir)
> I did not well, I meant well: all my Services
> You have pay'd home. But that you have vouchsaf'd
> (With your Crown'd Brother, and these your
> contracted
> Heires of your Kingdomes) my poore House to visit;
> It is a surplus of your Grace, which never
> My life may last to answere.
>
> (V. iii. 1)

In the first eight and a half lines occur "have had . . .", "did/ not/ well . . .", "have . . .", "have . . .", "is . . .", "may". In two short speeches there is a glide from a remote Pluperfect to the Present, ending with a hint of the Future in 'may'. Leontes retraces his Past, but retraces it to connect with a point from which he can advance to a position otherwise beyond his powers to reach.

But before the drawing of the curtain in l. 20, and in preparation for it, a curious postulate is raised. Leontes, who has yet to see the statue (which is a dummy of opposite kind to that which the Duchess of Malfi had shown to her, which was the live semblance of a dead person not, as here, the dead semblance of a live person), is told by Paulina about this work of art. She says of it:

> As she liv'd peerelesse,
> So her dead likenesse I doe well beleeve
> Excells what ever yet you look'd upon.

She insinuates the verb 'believe'. Now belief is that faculty which can translate the Mood of Subjunctive desire into the Mood of Indicative actuality.

Only after the voluntary act of believing has been introduced, as a power to modify a given situation, is the curtain drawn, and Leontes presented with a challenge. He exclaims:

> Chide me (deare Stone) that I *may say* indeed
> Thou *art* Hermione.

He is dared to believe the apparent is real; that what is desired is true. He does, and the play achieves its end as the Subjunctive Verb in the first line of the quotation becomes the Indicative Verb of the second.

Paulina had said "It is requir'd/You doe awake your Faith" as a condition for further marvels. Through the thickening Subjunctives: "If I had thought the sight . . . Would thus have wrought you" . . .; "Lest your Fancie/May think anon, it moves"; . . . "Would I were dead, but that . . ."; . . . "Would you not deeme it breath'd?" . . .; "The very Life seemes warme . . .", the translation is effected by and through the Imperatives of mere human command:

> Musick; awake her: Strike:
> 'Tis time: descend: be Stone no more: approach:
> Strike all that looke upon with mervaile: Come:
> Ile fill your Grave up: stirre: nay, come away:
> Bequeath to Death your numnesse: (for from him,
> Deare Life redeemes you) . . .

And they continue: "Start not"; "doe not shun her . . ." "present your Hand".

Whatever we feel about this scene, whether we find it convincing or whether we consider it savours too much of a stunt, we must yet recognize that a manipulation of Tense and Mood was essential for the achievement of its aim.

5 ADDITIONAL REMARKS

What we have been considering above is not the assumption that in Shakespeare's early plays, excepting the Chronicle Plays, the span of the total series of outward events shown on the stage can be supposed to take place within a shorter period of time than those in his late plays. Such an assumption would be demonstrably false. For although the events of *Romeo and Juliet* or *A Midsummer Night's Dream* take place in a few days, and the events of *The Winter's Tale* or *Pericles* take place over many years, yet the events of *The Merchant of Venice* presuppose a considerable, though vaguely-realized, period of time for their performance while all that happens in *The Tempest* is presumed to have occurred in a period of time actually shorter than is required to represent them on the stage. What we have been discussing is not the duration of stage-represented happenings—whether these are continuous or not—but the wide differences of temporal and modal apprehension as revealed by different phases of Shakespeare's career. With respect to its vastness of active memory and the scale on which it envisages future possibilities, *The Tempest* is only to be compared with *The Winter's Tale*, even though its plot takes place in less than the two hours needed to show it. Ultimately, we are dealing with qualitative differences of verse. Though the generosity of the hind- and fore-sight in *The Tempest* is the creation of all the elements in the poetry combined, yet Verb Forms are the agents which most immediately and practically work this result. Memorial resonance, the sense of the cumulate of an experience whose elements exist in varying, yet ever shifting, perspectives of a recession, can only be communicated by subtle handling of Tense; a distensible sense of possibility by a control of grammatical Moods.

Here the measure of Shakespeare's development herein can be demonstrated well enough by setting a piece of the exposition from *The Comedy of Errors* beside a passage, whose practical function is the same, from *The Tempest*.

In Act I, sc. i of *The Comedy of Errors* there is that long and dreary recital of his past by Egeon which is yet needed by the audience if they are to understand the events on the stage which they are soon to see. It begins:

> In Syracusa was I borne, and wedde
> Unto a woman, happy but for me,
> And by me; had not our hap beene bad:
> With her I liv'd in joy, our wealth increast
> By prosperous voyages I often made
> To Epidamium, till my factors death,
> And the great care of goods at randome left,
> Drew me from kinde embracements of my spouse;
> From whom my absence was not sixe moneths olde,
> Before her selfe (almost at fainting under
> The pleasing punishment that women beare)
> Had made provision for her following me,
> And soone, and safe, arrived where I was. . . .

but, though it carries on thus for another forty-six lines, I

75

forbear quoting further. Sufficient it is, I think, to note: (i) that the whole of this speech is fixedly set in the past by the speaker. What he reports is framed in a uniform Past Tense from which the speaker is now disengaged. The substance of what he says will explain the ensuing plot, but since it is not actively alive in Egeon, it will not modify the way in which the plot is beheld by the audience nor modify Egeon's own conduct within it; and (ii) the rigidity of Egeon's past, which appears as a numbered sequence of events between which no mutual interaction exists, follows from the speaker's sole dependence on two Tenses—the Perfect and, as in l. 3 of the quotation, the remoter Pluperfect. Both, as it were, in being perfected cease to act on the present. In practical terms, this lack of enterprise in the use of inflexions prevents the speech from having those variations of speed and sound, as well as of meanings, which the effective use of contrasting Verb Forms assure.

Compare the foregoing speech with a passage of dialogue from *The Tempest* (I. ii). It serves the same function, that of exposition, as Egeon's, and the substance or content of the two passages is similar. Both Egeon and Prospero tell their own stories of hard luck, sea-travel, exile; both tell of parent and child relations. That Egeon's patient stage audience listens with silent interest, while Miranda yawns, does not mean so much that the substance of Prospero's tale is more inherently boring—though, if Egeon and Prospero were offering their memoirs to the Sunday papers, an editor might well decide that Egeon had the more 'eventful', and so more interesting, 'Life', to sell—as that Shakespeare in *The Tempest* is hugely aware, after long practice, that exposition is an exacting challenge. By making Miranda somnolent he is forestalling objections from the audience. Moreover, the Duke in *The Comedy of Errors* is a stooge, receiving a discharge of information really meant for the audience; but Miranda is mediative. What she hears gives her a history and so alters her; what the audience hear, directly and through her, is plot data, but they also receive history of the teller, of the listener, and the background of the present shipwreck. Moreover, the mode adopted in *The Tempest* whereby Prospero, in his exploration of the "dark-backward and Abisme of time", also recalls what has been experienced by Miranda, though without her knowledge, means that Shakespeare is enabled to use a range of Pronouns denied to Egeon:

> I thus neglecting worldly ends, all dedicated
> To closenes, and the bettering of my mind
> With that, which but by being so retir'd
> Ore-priz'd all popular rate: in my false brother
> Awak'd an evill nature, and my trust
> Like a good parent, did beget of him
> A falsehood in it's contrarie, as great
> As my trust was, which had indeede no limit,
> A confidence sans bound. He being thus Lorded,
> Not onely with what my revenew yeelded,
> But what my power might els exact. Like one
> Who having minted truth, by telling of it,
> Made such a synner of his memorie
> To credite his owne lie, he did beleeve
> He was indeed the Duke, out o'th' Substitution
> And executing th' outward face of Roialtie
> With all prerogative: hence his Ambition growing: . . .
>   (I. ii. 88)

Prospero's story has a life and authority which Egeon's had not. This tick, this life lies—some would say—in the movement of the verse. It does, but that movement is accomplished by the beat, variation, time-changing semantics (or meanings) of the Verbs. These change their Tense, Mood, and so force a listener or reader to change his gear of knowledge and to shift his perspectives. These verbs are, in the order he hears them: the Present Indicative (twice); the Present Participle; the Past Participle; the "Ore-priz'd" with its force; the Past Tense ("awaked", carries stress at head of line); the "did beget", a continuous Past; the pathetic Pluperfect "had"; "being" with its force beside the just-preceding "had"; the deceptive Subjunctive of the next pair of lines; the Past Tense; and the Present Participle (twice).

Our next quotation is shorter:

> Whereon
> A treacherous Armie levied, one mid-night
> Fated to th' purpose, did Anthonio open

> The gates of Millaine, and ith' dead of darkenesse
> The ministers for th' purpose hurried thence
> Me, and thy crying selfe.

where the 'perfected' is yanked into the Present by the auxiliary "did" which is divided by "Anthonio" from the "open" (which is immediate, now) it governs; and the "hurried" resurrects the urgency of a gone time, an urgency reinforced by the "crying".

Finally:

> In few, they hurried us a-boord a Barke,
> Bore us some Leagues to Sea, where they prepared
> A rotten carkasse of a Butt, not rigg'd,
> Nor tackel, sayle, nor mast, the very rats
> Instinctively *have quit* it: There they *hoyst*[1] *us*
> *To cry* to th' Sea, that roard to us; to sigh
> To th' windes, whose pitty sighing backe againe
> Did us but loving wrong.

There, in seven and a half lines, the Past curves into what is, for Prospero, an enduring Present in line 5, and then curves back again to the Past: a boomerang thrown into memory. Though Prospero may not *have done* so much as Egeon, he *is doing* more with what he did.

Comparative work on grammatical usage at different periods needs to be done but, purely provisionally, it would seem that Shakespeare's so-called 'progress' depended—and this is neither original nor claims to be so—on his developing power to harness (or, in other, but tired, words: to increasingly realize) a naturally growing experience. So. But experience is acquired in and through time (we pass "through nature to eternity", etc.) and in no way else. And this experience, or time-travelling, standardly incurs—for him, for us—a demolition of belief in a Continuous or Platonic Present. But Shakespeare went on through various actual, or indicative, Present-Past or Past-Present formulae to arrive at—*because* he could say it—a knowledge of the Subjunctive become fact.

Naturally (again), by experience (something acquired, or

---

[1] I am aware that 'hoist' also occurs as a Past in early seventeenth-century English.

put upon us, in time) we also mean, primarily—since the Middle Ages—experience, not of Wordsworth's mountains, nor of God's nor anyone's Nature, but of—and *with*, and *by*, and *from*, and *through*—men and women. We know the name, love, given to that multiplicity. That, however, is incidental, except to remind us that in the conjugations 'to love', 'to die', 'to hope' or 'to despair', the Personal Pronouns figure on the page of our English Grammar and determine the inflexions of the verbs they govern. I have hinted at the relevance of this in my section on the *Sonnets*. If I have neglected the problem of the choice of Pronouns in the plays, it is because we shall next concentrate briefly on the part played by this Part of Speech in the work of some of Shakespeare's contemporaries.

IV   Elizabethan and Jacobean
'Personal' Insights

I   PRONOUNS IN 'THE REVENGER'S TRAGEDY'

I SHALL take it that it is possible to date *The Revenger's Tragedy* and *The Atheist's Tragedy* 1607 and 1609, respectively. This puts them in an interesting relation with Shakespeare's *Coriolanus* and *Antony and Cleopatra* and with Jonson's *Volpone* and *Epicœne*. I shall further assume, though it is not utterly material to my argument, that the traditional ascription of *The Revenger's Tragedy* to Tourneur is correct. Despite the claims made on behalf of Middleton, notably by Dr. Samuel S. Schoenbaum,[1] my intuitive belief that *The Revenger's Tragedy* issued from the same mind as that which composed *The Atheist's Tragedy* remains unshaken; and this belief receives the strongest intellectual support from Inga-Stina Ekeblad's new evidence on behalf of Tourneur.[2]

"Thou shell of Death" (I. i. 18[3]): Vindice addresses the skull which was once "the bright face" of his "betrothed Lady" as 'thou'. This mode of address, as distinct from 'you' is appropriate if to Tourneur 'you' is still charged with the notion of plurality. He can be compared with the Shakespeare of the *Sonnets* who turned or advanced the word 'you' to denote not plurality of persons but the plurality—body *and* soul—of

---

[1] See *Middleton's Tragedies* (Yale University Press, 1954).

[2] See "The Authorship of *The Revenger's Tragedy*", *English Studies*, forthcoming.

[3] References are to *The Works of Cyril Tourneur* edited by Allardyce Nicoll (London, The Fanfrolico Press, undated).

which a single person is compounded.[1] Tourneur seems as conservative in his grammatical habits as he was in his cast of thought: the conservatism of the one involved, or was one with, conservatism in the other. Moreover, Tourneur here uses 'thou' because 'thou' implies formality and not, as might at first thought be expected, intimacy. It is a distancing word and his mistress, Gloriana, is now as distant from Vindice as can be—by the stroke of death. What is now an 'it' was once part of 'her':

> . . . thou shell of Death,
> Once the bright face of my betrothed Lady,
> When life and beauty naturally fild out
> These ragged imperfections . . .

To point an extreme contrast: Vindice is not near a whole living person compounded of body and soul as Florizel is when he is with Perdita at the opening of *The Winter's Tale*, Act IV, sc. iv. There Shakespeare makes Florizel address Perdita as 'you'. This in the plays (leaving aside the *Sonnets*) is the rarer usage in Shakespeare when it is a single person who is the object of address. But it is justified by the circumstances mentioned. There it has special force.[2]

Yet it must not be concluded that *number* was a finally exclusive determinant governing Tourneur's choice of pronouns. Conservative as he was, other considerations played their part to the modification of this rule. For while Tourneur agrees with Shakespeare in addressing but a part of a single person, living or dead, or but an aspect of a personality, as 'thou', he can also agree with Shakespeare in using 'you' when the whole of a person, conceived as a multiple, is spoken to, or even when it would seem that it is the *innermost* part of one who is being addressed. Thus, in the dialogue that follows the lines we have quoted, the brothers, Vindice and Hippolito, change from addressing each other as 'thou' to 'you'. But 'you' makes its first appearance in this scene, where Vindice is concerned, when he touches Hippolito home—as with a rapier—or to the quick with his "I reach you, for I know . . ."

[1] See III above, especially p. 42.
[2] See above, p. 72. Richard Flatter (*Shakespeare's Producing Hand*) in his note on Shakespeare's use of 'thou' and 'you' would seem to follow E. A. Abbott, quoted above, p. 37.

(I. i. 90). (Hippolito has used it before; but then he is appealing for recognition as a brother.) The change is then significant; it marks a change in relations between the brothers, a change to swift directions in place of a slower, more elaborate, formality.

In the most famous or infamous scene of *The Revenger's Tragedy* (Act III, sc. v[1]) the pronouns 'thou' and 'you', and their accompanying possessive adjectives, have a great significance, especially when one remembers that on every occasion where a stage person was addressing but one other stage person, Tourneur—like Shakespeare—had a choice between 'thou' ('thy' and 'thine') and 'you' ('your' and 'yours'). What are the specific reasons—dramatic, poetic, psychological—behind each specific choice?

At the outset of Act III, sc. v Vindice—wildly excited over his plot and certainly pleased with himself for inventing it— withholds the 'you' mode of address from his brother. Hippolito is in the inferior position. He asks to know the cause of Vindice's elation, and then strengthens his appeal by the use of the more intimately personal pronoun. Vindice, after first teasing and tantalizing with the distancing, more formal, slightly chilling 'thee', in the manner of one who returns 'Good evening' to a too assuming, too impertinently familiar 'Hello', later relents. But first: "Ile divide it to thee", he says, about to satisfy the curiosity he has aroused. Then he tells his plot. Now that he has been 'divided to', Hippolito becomes a 'you'— partner. Yet still there's no real equality. Vindice by the retention of additional knowledge keeps the beseeching Hippolito at a disadvantage:

> *Vindice:* . . . You cannot finde me yet (i.e. 'you still don't
> know all, by a long way')
> I'me in a throng of happy Apprehensions.
> Hee's suted for a Lady; I haue tooke care
> For a delitious lip, a sparkling eye—
> *You* shall be witnesse brother;
> Be ready, stand with your hat off.
>
> (III. v. 32)

Kind but condescending. How self-flattering to be in a position to tell someone something they don't know! But—dramatically

---

[1] In the Mermaid edition, the scene is numbered Act III, sc. iv.

—the pronominal choices, Vindice's concessive 'you's', and his readiness to withdraw them at each stiffening of his pride, reflect and express the relative position of Vindice and Hippolito *vis-à-vis* each other, within the plot, throughout.

Presently (l. 46), Vindice addresses "the skull of his love drest up in Tires". Now the object of these exciting addresses demands a dual approach. She or it is two persons or things. On the one hand she commands a 'thou' as the *memento mori*, the traditional medieval emblem, magisterial in her sign. What anchorite could be so flippant as to breathe out a 'you' to this emblem of the great unifier, Death? Thus, when he removes the mask to expose what is beneath, the singular becomes instantly appropriate: "Art thou beguild now?" (l. 52). Yet up to the moment of this 'exposure' she—'she' here, more than an 'it'—had been a 'stand-in', a dummy for one who, were she but living, would have had the intimate nearness to him which she had in the past and for which 'you' is appropriate:

> 'Tis the best grace you haue to do it well.
> Ile saue your hand that labour; Ile vnmaske you.

But so "beguild", the 'you' who was once Vindice's mistress and who, disguised, is now to become the Duke's and who is, or was, at any rate a 'Lady', becomes 'thou'. 'Thou' is proper to this "thing", to refine which "yon fellow" falsifies highways. Thus:

> Do's the Silke-worme expend her yellow labours
> For thee? for thee dos she vndoe herselfe?

The skull is now consistently addressed as 'thou', its role as emblem of death is now dominant. But the pronominal forms applied to others involved in this scene—whether they be 'characters' or audience—show the similar discrimination. Thus, for example, the collected female members of the Globe audience are addressed from the stage by Vindice under the plural 'you'. Indicating the dolled-up *memento mori* he says:

> See Ladies, with false formes
> *You* deceiue men, but cannot deceiue wormes.

With the entry of the Duke there is a complication. As a royal personage, or ruler, he refers to himself as 'we', or objectively as 'us', and in return receives the polite forms of 'you'

83

and 'your'. In fact he is so politely—or with studied or ironic obsequiousness—addressed up to the moment he has kissed the skull of Gloriana (l. 152). Then, with the Duke irremediably poisoned and soon to die, Vindice switches from the polite plural (Pronoun and Verb-inflection) to the goad of a second personal singular, hostile, mocking, vindictive. It is a turn from the 'polite': "Your grace knowes now what you haue to doo", to the triumphing and bullying insolence of

> Brother—place the Torch here, that his affrighted eyeballs
> May start into those hollowes. Duke, dost knowe
> Yon dreadfull vizard? view it well, tis the skull
> Of *Gloriana*, whom thou poysonedst last.

(III. v. 155)

And until his intensifying agony is at last over, he is pointedly 'thou-ed' and 'thy-ed', insistently and with rising emphasis. The fallen enemy is being 'crowed over'.[1] It is true that amid this accumulative cluster of 'thou's' and 'thy's', the polite 'you' and 'your' is used sometimes. But perhaps it is not too fanciful to suppose that these departures are also deliberate and dramatic; that they are also uttered with a special emphasis: the emphasis and intonation of biting sarcasm applied to his 'slavish' Dukeship. Moreover, the first two instances of this here *falsely* polite form are immediately followed by a revival to the impolite inflexion and Vindice's sudden revelation of his identity:

Duke: My teeth are eaten out.
Vindice: Hadst any left?
Hippolito: I thinke but few.
Vindice: Then those that did eate are eaten.
Duke: O my tongue.
Vindice: *Your* tongue? twill teach *you* to kiss closer,
Not like a Slobbering Dutchman—*you* haue eyes still:
Looke monster, what a Lady hast *thou* made me,
My once betrothed wife.

Duke: Is it thou villaine? nay then—
Vindice: 'Tis I, 'tis Vindice, 'tis I.

(III. v. 169; italics mine)

---

[1] One is reminded of the cruel taunting by Sir Edward Coke, of Sir Walter Raleigh at his trial: "All that he did was at thy Instigation, thou viper; for I *thou* thee, thou Traitor."

Selecting but a couple of test situations, or scenes, from *The Revenger's Tragedy* (admittedly, they are two such where contrasting and changing levels, or perspectives, among the personal relationships between the characters, needed to be prominently defined by the dramatist), we can say that Tourneur, at least sometimes, functionally discriminates between the two Pronouns of the Second Person which he has at his disposal. Being, as we have said, as conservative in language as in thought, he does not perhaps evolve new meanings of his pronouns, pioneering new kinds of human relationships, as does Shakespeare. Nevertheless, he uses 'thou' with one range of meaning, and 'you' with another. These are traditional, and traditionally distinct, ranges—a distinction he can intensify through irony or sarcasm. In Tourneur 'thou' conveys one way in which a human being can regard another person or thing, while 'you' conveys another. These words are therefore keys opening to the nature of different relationships; and so, if Tourneur makes a speaker change from 'thou' to 'you', or *vice versa*, then the change signifies a change in the relationship between the speaker and the person, or the personalized thing, spoken to. Such changes in relationships can be either in the nature of changes of 'level' or changes of perspective. Where Tourneur, in *The Revenger's Tragedy*, seems most fluctuating in his use of the two words is in the relationship between Vindice and Hippolito. But here the fluctuation is also purposeful, and helps to define Vindice as the leader of the two. Vindice, by his use of pronouns, is arrogant and patronizing; Hippolito, often snubbed, aspires to equality.

As the last quotation from the play shows, we may be ready to expect, in the Elizabethan Drama, that when any 'character' throws off his disguise and discovers himself to another 'character', then the new level or perspective of relationship thereby created is accompanied, and in part created, by a change in pronoun.

Finally, the subtilty of the pronouns in *The Revenger's Tragedy*, in the scenes we have discussed, suggests that we have, after further examination of the usage of this Part of Speech in Elizabethan-Jacobean drama, an instrument which we can employ to help determine certain questions of authorship—not least that of *The Revenger's Tragedy* itself in its relation to *The*

Atheist's Tragedy on the one hand and the tragedies of Middleton on the other.

2   DONNE AND THE SINGULAR

I said earlier that Donne was our most conspicuous 'I-Thou' poet.[1] A re-reading of *The Songs and Sonets* alone confirms this, though this is not of course surprising since these poems are nearly all concerned with, or are poetic records of, the love relationship of Donne—the 'I'—and a Woman—the 'Thou'. For Donne hardly ever speaks *about* the Woman in the Third Person in the manner of King's "Tell me no more how fair she is", rather he speaks directly *to* her. But, though it is conceded that a lover directly addressing his mistress provides the clearest possible situation, the supreme type of situation whatever the period or language, where the antimeric 'I'—'Thou' might be expected,[2] yet—in point of fact—Donne (since he had already ruled out the third person 'she', an initial choice which was to make him the kind of poet he is) next had the choice, as had Shakespeare in the *Sonnets*, between using 'thou' and 'you'. That Donne, with a few interesting exceptions, insists on 'thou', raises questions which it is the task of this section to attempt to answer. Was the 'modern' Donne being grammatically conservative? Because he was addressing in his *Songs and Sonets* one woman—or, at least, one woman at a time— did he therefore use the Singular Form of the Pronoun? Or is the stress on 'thou' one of specifically poetic intention rather than of grammatical reason? For certainly the word is extraordinarily stressed—by its rhythmic positioning, by the weight of meaning it bears, and by its sheer frequency in the *Songs and Sonets* regarded as a whole. Was not Donne, instead of being subservient to the laws of Grammar, being particularly enterprising in an exploration of the full possibilities of 'thou'-ness in a way a poet today could not without at once disqualifying himself for using an antiquated word?

[1] See above, p. 37.

[2] Against which it might be urged that the love relationship between a man and a god provides the real 'type'. The Book of Common Prayer, the Psalms, writers of Hymns and Donne in his Divine Poems, address, of course, a 'Thou'. The fact is, love is *singular* in intent, whether directed to *a* god, *a* man or *a* woman, to this parent or that, to this child or that child.

In attempting to answer such questions, we should, I think, initially recognize that, while we are bound to respect the cautions of Sir Herbert Grierson and of others on the subject, it is still possible to assume that the poems comprising *Songs and Sonets* are arranged in a significant order, an order which traces a love, or an 'I-thou' experience, through various stages—from its inception, on and through to its *poetic* expiry. But if *Songs and Sonets*, like a diary, tell a story, there is no need to assume further that the individual poems were necessarily *composed* in the order of their final arrangements. And one would have to admit to the existence of a few poems which do not easily fit into the story, such as those which address women other than the particular mistress[1] (for Donne, our most effrontingly 'masculine' poet, was enough a man to be able to be interested in more than one woman over a period of years despite his general constancy), and to the existence of others on the amatory theme in general.

Apart from these, confessedly important exceptions, we repeat it is still reasonable to suppose that *Songs and Sonets* charts the course and duration of an 'affair', Donne's relationship, with one particular woman, from the first surprising discovery of the 'thou' and 'I' of

> I Wonder by my troth, what thou and I
> Did, till we lov'd?[2]

with the novel 'we'-ness thence derived or born, to the tired and much-knowing end of the affair (poetically the end) expressed by *The Paradox, Farewell to Love, A Lecture Upon the Shadow, The Token*, and lastly the caustic and narrowly appraising *Selfe Love*.

Now, moving within that well-travelled rhythm from discovery (or first infatuation) to rejection and newly-won independence, Donne speaks to the 'thou' directly, though not necessarily aggressively, but on the level—in a tone appropriate to the level—of an equal. There is, in Donne, none of that humility we find in the earlier and middle sonnets of Shakespeare, where the 'I'—the identity of the writer—seems

---

[1] I am especially thinking here of that profoundly moving poem, *A Nocturnall Upon S. Lucies Day*.

[2] I quote from Sir Herbert Grierson's edition.

lost in contemplation of an adored at once both remote and superior. Donne assumes that he is on the same plane as his mistress, though he has the initiative on that plane through belonging to the superior (as the Schoolmen would have taught him) sex.[1] The 'I' is as important to Donne as the 'thou'; it is the 'I' who discovers the 'thou'. From the combination of his 'I' and the 'thou' he discovers something which proceeds from them. Together, the souls of 'I' and 'thou' result not in a merely additive mixture, but in a new birth, or soul, which is neither the one nor the other, nor yet the two simply added together; but is

> That abler soule, which thence doth flowe,

and which

> Defects of lonelinesse controules.

Thus Donne, as a poet, in exploring the 'I-thou' relationship, struggles to express the pronoun signifying that relationship. But though the meaning exists, there is no word for it, neither Noun nor Pronoun. The Pronoun he sought, whose meaning he tried to, and perhaps did, define, was not the simple, or additive, plural 'we', which stands for any number of persons upwards of two (though what is then assumed to be *shared* can be of the smallest, most precarious or, even, an unreal kind, but the word signifying that dual or exclusive 'we-two'-ness which perhaps only lovers can know. Now, a thousand years or more before Donne there had indeed been, according to Joseph Wright, a word, a Pronoun, existing which precisely conveyed this state, as exclusive of others as it is inclusive of those to whom it refers, namely the old dual Pronoun of 'we-two'-ness, 'wit'.[2] This Pronoun meant more than just 'we

---

[1] He speaks thus, but this freedom implies that the affair has gone on for some time. Though he may have begun by worshipping, that stage is past. *The Good-morrow* remembers the beginning of a relationship from a later position where the freedom of equality has been attained.

[2] " 'Wit' (Goth., O.S. wit) and 'git' (O.S. git) were unaccented plurals with the addition of -t which is of obscure origin. There are grave phonological difficulties against assuming that the -t is related to the numeral for two." Joseph Wright, *Old English Grammar*, 3rd edition, p. 241. Traces of the dual of the First Person are found as late as in *Layamon* and in the *Owl and the Nightingale*. See H. C. Wyld, *A Short History of English*, 3rd edition, p. 228.

two': it expressed the particular will of lovers when one spoke
in the assurance that he spoke for both. Now Donne was de-
prived, by its regrettable extinction, of the Pronoun which
spoke for a special state of being, yet he does what he can to
restore its *meaning* by poetic inflexion. Thus, in

> I Wonder by my troth, what thou, and I
> Did, till we lov'd? were we not wean'd till then?

the lost Dual Pronoun of the First Person—for which today
'we', which must either be whispered or be offensive, has to do
service—with its powerful and essential sense of exclusiveness,
is recovered and defined not by formal grammatical inflexion
but by poetic emphasis, that is periphrasis. For in order to
ask the question 'where was wit before wit was born?' Donne
is compelled to resort to enumerating its previous constituents:
'I and thou'. But we need not, it might be said, be sorry that
Donne had to depend on such shifts—one must term them
poetic inflexions—in order to create the meaning of a single
lost Pronoun since it led to such results as:

> She is all States, and all Princes, I,
> Nothing else is,

which is exactly a statement of the mystery of 'wit'-ness. Thus,
while Donne is the great 'I-thou' poet, he is also sovereign in
creating a special *restricted* 'we'—unknown to Shakespeare of the
Sonnets—and a condition required for this was a concentration
on the uniqueness of 'thou' (for, to Donne, the 'you' had still
an ineradicable residual meaning of plurality), for it was the
singular 'thou' *plus* the 'I' which constituted, for him, 'wit'.

The exceptions to 'thou', the few cases of its apparent alternative, 'you', and its possessive derivatives, in *Songs and Sonets*
consequently stand out. The first occurs in *Womans Constancy*.
Beginning with the 'thou' there is the pointed change to the
other form:

> Now thou hast lov'd me one whole day,
> To morrow when thou leav'st, what wilt thou say?
> Wilt thou then Antedate some new made vow?
>   Or say that now
> We are not just those persons, which we were?
> Or, that oathes made in reverentiall feare
> Of Love, and his wrath, any may forsweare?

> Or, as true deaths, true maryages untie,
> So lovers contracts, images of those,
> Binde but till sleep, deaths image, them unloose?
> Or, *your* owne end to Justifie,
> For having purpos'd change, and falsehood; *you*
> Can have no way but falsehood to be true?
> Vaine lunatique, against these scapes I could
> Dispute, and conquer, if I would,
> Which I abstaine to doe,
> For by to morrow, I may thinke so too.

The italics are mine, but they point what is surely the case —that just as the 'thou' is certainly stressed, for consider the insistency of its repetition and its cross-rhyming with 'vow' and 'now', so are the 'your' and 'you' when the change in Pronouns occurs. The change in pronouns registers a change of attitudes, almost a *volte face*. Something might be allowed to the need to find a rhyme to 'true'. But we are concerned with the result, and the very fact that it is a rhyme-word helps to lay the emphasis on the 'you'. But the purpose of the change is clear. Donne alters his attitude to her because by tomorrow she will have altered her attitude to him. She will no longer be the singular 'thou', a partner in 'wit', but one of the commonalty of women to whom he can attribute words: "you will justify yourself by saying this and this". Addressed as 'you' she becomes distanced, one of those whom he could include in the terms of *The Indifferent*:

> I can love her, and her, and you and you,
> I can love any, so she be not true.

Elsewhere in *Songs and Sonets* Donne uses 'you' in a curious, exact, and peculiarly scholastic sense which I call the 'combinative'. In two of the poems there is a switch from an initial 'thou' to a 'you' and a final return to 'thou'. But examination shows that in these instances of 'you' there is an underlying signification of plurality. For example in these lines from *The Legacie*:

> I heard mee say, Tell her anon,
> That my selfe, (that is you, not I,)
> Did kill me . . .

Donne is saying that the 'I' and 'thou' are *also* each the other, that each has become plural. So he is addressing both himself and her, combined in her person, when he says:

> It kill'd mee againe, that I who still was true,
> In life, in my last Will should cozen you.

Similarly in *A Valediction: of my Name, in the Window*, the 'you' is combinative:

> Then, as all my soules bee,
> Emparadis'd in *you*, (in whom alone
> I understand, and grow and see,)
> The rafters of my body, bone
> Being still with you, the Muscle, Sinew, and Veine,
> Which tile this house, will come againe.

Donne in addressing her is also addressing himself who is in her, and that makes two, following from the earlier statement at the conclusion of the second stanza of the same poem, "I am you". The same mechanism of thought operates in *The Flea*. Because it had "suck'd me first, and now sucks thee,/And in this flea, our two bloods mingled bee", the insect is next addressed as a combinative 'you'.

Finally, enough has been said, I think, to indicate that in the opening line of *The Canonization*:

> For Godsake hold your tongue, and let me love,

a generalized plural is meant. Donne is addressing all and sundry outside 'wit'. He is not telling his mistress to leave off talking so that he can get to work with caresses, instead he is telling the rest of the world to stop preaching to him about the advisability of giving his time to other affairs than love.

When he comes to address the Eternal God instead of a human mistress, Donne is equally meticulous in his choice of Pronouns. Except when he is explicitly addressing the Trinity, which is for him plural, as in:

> Batter my heart, three person'd God; for, you
> As yet but knocke, breathe, shine, and seeke to mend,

he uses 'thou', not only in consequence of pious custom and literal rendering of Number as observed in the Latin of the Catholic liturgy to which he had been bred, but also because in the passion of his devotion to God he was still exploring a singular 'thou'-ness with as much fervour as when a mistress had been the object of his devotion. Admitting that Donne, thanks to his training in scholastic philosophy, was more rigorous than other poets in his respect for the logic of Grammar, yet his poetic perception of the mystery of Number additionally guarantees that his choice with respect to Pronouns is never merely conventional or merely 'poetical' (as with many nineteenth-century poets) or merely haphazard. Rather he realizes afresh a traditional discrimination between two forms.

The one section of his verse where Donne might seem most regardless of whether he uses 'thou' or 'you' is in his *Verse Letters*. But compare the forms he uses there with those in the Prose Letters, and it is evident that they are indices of the degree of acquaintance he owed to his correspondents. To his familiar friends he uses 'thou'; to those above himself in station (or to those he knows less well) he uses 'you'. But since his usage here reflects social convention more narrowly, and since these occasional poems in any case have a limited poetic purpose, it is to the *Songs and Sonets* and the *Divine Poems* that we must look for an individually significant discrimination between 'thou' and 'you'. For Donne, as a poet, put most of himself in those poems where he spoke to one other person— whether a mistress or God—on that which most intensely concerned him: the experience of love.

3 BEAUMONT AND FLETCHER: SOME LOST DISTINCTIONS

Whereas of Shakespeare and Tourneur and Donne it can be said that each had distinguished between the Second Person Pronouns 'thou' and 'you' in their different ways, depending on their individual sensibilities, their perception of another's personality, and their understanding of Number (however much they disagreed among themselves about these matters the three of them agreeing in recognizing a difference between the two forms), of Beaumont and Fletcher it must be admitted that while they recognize a distinction they are careless in its application. When a dramatist has two words to imply contrasting ways of regarding a person then he has (at least) a powerful psychological advantage at his disposal in the creation and ordering of his drama. Yet the very casualness with which Beaumont and Fletcher use this resource actually contributes to the interest these dramatists have as symptoms of their times. Their drama illustrates a society in which distinctions were becoming blurred.

In *Philaster*, for example, a play which is dated around 1608, and belongs therefore to the years when the more 'old-fashioned' *thou* might be supposed to be yielding to the more 'fashionable' *you*, irrespective of Number, 'you' does, in fact, greatly predominate. Yet there is no consistency. Hence in Act I, sc. ii, Arethusa follows up the question "What will you do, Philaster, with *your* self?" with the advice "Dear, hide *thy* self".[1] With the change of Pronoun there is no change in relations. They remain at the same psychological distance, and on the same plane, with respect to each other. The change of Pronoun does not mark a breach in the guard against intimacy or a retreat of the affections—*daunger* remains inactive; nor does the change signify that Arethusa suddenly arrives at a new insight into the personality of Philaster, though a reading of the whole scene is necessary to see the justice of these remarks. One must simply suppose that one of the collaborators has slipped into using the form common in his boyhood but now growing rarer in favour of the more 'modish' *you*. But which collaborator? Probably Beaumont. It is in the eight or so plays in which he is believed to have had an equal or dominating share that the 'thou's' chiefly occur. Since he was the younger of the two that might seem surprising. Yet his mind, though bold, had a sturdiness absent in Fletcher, and this retention of forms which once had vitality is perhaps a sign of this sturdiness. Working alone, he might have used the word as a specific discriminating instrument in the analysis of personal relations: but in collaboration its presence is vestigial rather than functional.

Yet as a passage of some length is likely to prove a fairer test than a couple of lines, we will next turn to Act I, sc. i and

[1] *Works*, edited by A. Glover and A. R. Waller, Vol. I, pp. 88 and 89. In this edition the lines are not numbered.

Act I, sc. ii of *The Maid's Tragedy*. These provide us with situations in which a number of persons speak. It is true that the range in social scale covered by these persons is the narrow one typical of Beaumont and Fletcher, extending as it does merely from the King to his attendant lords and ladies. Yet within this group, with its homogeneity of tastes and manners, the relationships are intricate and rapidly changing in consequence of the elaborate intrigue of the—again highly typical—plot. Surely some of the many readjustments in personal relations, resulting from these artful manipulations of plot, call for pronominal signals—if only for the guidance of the audience —to mark these changes and shifts? Moreover, in the first of these scenes there is a masque. Do the maskers address each other in forms distinguishable from those used by their 'stage-audience'?

In the first of the scenes Calianax and Diagoras,[1] two testy old men, address each other as 'you' up to a point—that point is where Calianax has worked himself up to a quivering rage and is desirous of being particularly insulting, thus:

Calianax: My looks terrifie them, you Coxcombly Ass *you*!
  I'le be judg'd by all the company whether *thou* hast not a
  worse face than I——[2]

When Melantius enters he uses 'you' so long as he is equable. But when this bluff soldier, who is uncertain of temper like Shakespeare's Falconbridge, of whom he is in the line of descent, has his wrath aroused by Calianax, the father of that Aspatia who has been jilted in favour of Evadne, Melantius' sister, Melantius 'thou's' him unmercifully.[3] But becoming tender and compassionate he uses 'you' to his sister when she enters. Thus it would seem that a rule is being established: that in Beaumont and Fletcher the word of mutual regard is 'you', but that when ceremony and politeness are cast to the winds and the aim is to wound, then the 'thou' is invoked. Yet that is not so, for when the King enters he uses both forms with no apparent intention to discriminate.

Now during the masque, when such exalted mythological

---

[1] *Works*, Vol. I, p. 5. In the selection of Beaumont and Fletcher in the Everyman Series (Dent), the stage direction *Enter Calianax and Diagoras* initiates a new scene—viz. Act I, sc. ii. It is from this point in the play that my remarks apply. [2] *Ibid.*, p. 6. [3] *Ibid.*, p. 7.

deities as Night, Cynthia, Neptune and Eolus, speak, we might have expected a serious effort on the part of the dramatists to give them a consistent, highly formal mode of utterance so as to distinguish them from the 'audience within an audience'. Now the relation of this masque to the rest of the play in which it occurs is a matter beyond our scope, yet its tenuousness is suggested by the fact that these maskers twice *lapse* from the general—and, it would seem, intended—form of 'thou', but in each case there is no precise or subtle variation of meaning, either between the maskers themselves or in relation to their audience. In neither instance are they 'passing something under cover'.

Hopes that some sort of principle might yet inform the writers, despite earlier appearances, disappear in the nevertheless exciting and brilliant Act II, sc. i. Evadne, certainly, when nettled and peeved by Dula, appointed to undress her for the marriage-bed, tends to 'thou' her when irritated by the attendant's pointed innuendoes but, in the later dialogue between Evadne and Amintor, the forms 'thou' and 'you', though they are not regarded as synonyms, are used haphazardly.

It will be remembered that the King has commanded Amintor to break his troth to Aspatia and to marry Evadne. It grieves Amintor to desert Aspatia but the commands of the King, since he rules by Divine Right, are sacred and it would be heinous sin to disobey. On the night of his wedding he is ardent for his marital rights. Evadne refuses his advances. This is not due to "the coyness of a Bride", but because she is the King's mistress. He is to be a husband only in name and since he will never share Evadne's bed he has no sort of fair exchange for Aspatia, and yet for honour's sake he must, in public, put on an air of satisfaction. Here, in this extended passage of dialogue, the relation of Amintor with Evadne— his attitude towards her—undergoes subtle change as she slowly and cruelly removes the disguise of her appearance— discovers herself for what she is. Amintor begins with ecstatic anticipation of erotic bliss (that his marriage is by royal command and at the price of deserting Aspatia does not lessen this) and ends with the realization that he is the victim of a hoax. Much 'happens' between them. In the process, Amintor, it is true, *mostly* uses the Singular form in his pleading, as though he were conscious that this gave his speech a special pathos; while

Evadne *mostly* uses the Plural, as though it were an instrument with which she can keep Amintor at a distance. This is effective as far as it goes, and it may be the mark of one of the collaborators—probably Beaumont. But this is not sustained, and presently the two forms are used interchangeably. Yet even before this, while 'thou' and 'you' are being used as distinct words to some purpose, one suspects that the distinction has become narrowed to a point of etiquette. As in the French (*tu* as against *vous*) 'thou' simply betokens the intimacy Amintor is claiming; 'you' the formality which Evadne preserves against entreaty. Yet these are mere forms and the perception which once underlay them, and which gave the words an operancy over a wide area of human experience—on the evidence of Shakespeare in the *Sonnets*, of Donne in his love poems, of Tourneur in *The Revenger's Tragedy*—seems to have faded.

The verse of Fletcher, though not of Beaumont and Fletcher, shows a fondness for 'ye' in place of 'you'. Shakespeare also came to be attracted by this form and, apart from the humorously-wilful archaic 'ye's' in earlier work, used it in *The Tempest*. Shakespeare and Fletcher (or Fletcher alone,) then work its possibilities in *Henry VIII*. How far this interest in 'ye' was stimulated by the Authorized Version of 1611, and whether this Version made the form familiar to people of the kind who composed the dramatists' audience, we do not know. But whereas the Authorized Version employs 'ye' grammatically, that is only as a Nominative,[1] Fletcher, and Shakespeare, use it independent of respect to Case.

Here is an example from *The Tempest*—Caliban is cursing Prospero and Miranda:

> As wicked dewe, as ere my mother brush'd
> With Ravens feather from unwholesome Fen
> Drop on you both: A Southwest blow on yee,
> And blister you all ore.

> (I. ii. 318–21)

---

[1] "The Modern *you* is of course the old Dative. Caxton still uses *ye* for the Nominative and *you* only in oblique case. The sixteenth-century language of the Prayer Book, and the seventeenth-century language of the Authorized Version of the Bible, preserve the old distinction—e.g. 'Ye have not chosen me, but I have chosen you',"—H. C. Wyld, *A Short History of English*, p. 228.

Why, at the end of the third line quoted, "yee" in place of 'you'? For elsewhere Caliban addresses Prospero as 'you'. And why "yee" in place of the usual spelling of the Folio 'ye'? or the much rarer, though commoner than 'yee', 'y'?

Allowances must be made for capriciousness on the part of author or compositor. But when all allowances have been made, does not the spelling suggest that Shakespeare was directing the actor how to say the word? Longer than the customary 'ye', "yee" was to be heavily accented and uttered with the protracted mouth-splitting grin of implacable malice. The position of "yee" at the end of the line asks for this emphasis (cf. that other instance of "yee"—sonnet 42, l. 5). The comma, not required by logic or grammar, marks the pause before the actor relaxes his grimace. An edition of the play in standardized modern spelling conceals, of course, Shakespeare' intention.

In the next line "you" is said quickly and with no emphasis, the dramatic stress there falling on "ore".

But the form has advantages over 'you' in other kinds of context too:

> . . . for those you make friends,
> And give your hearts to; when they once perceive
> The least rub in your fortunes, fall away
> Like water from ye, never found againe
> But where they meane to sinke ye: all good people
> Pray for me, I must now forsake ye; the last houre
> Of my long weary life is come upon me:
> (*Henry VIII*, II. i. 27)

where the repeated unstressed—and here shortened—'ye' abundantly contributes to the limp, elegiac, falling-away effect which is aimed for and achieved.

Elsewhere we find:

> Now I feele
> Of what course Mettle ye are molded, Envy,
> How eagerly ye follow my Disgraces
> As if it fed ye, and how sleeke and wanton
> Ye appeare in every thing may bring my ruine?
> (*Henry VIII*, III. ii. 238)

where, as in the line "Vaine pompe, and glory of this World, I hate ye" (III. ii. 365), the pronoun 'ye', because of its Biblical, liturgical and homiletic associations, is appropriate for expressing a *contemptus mundi*. The Lords Suffolk and Surrey are being addressed by Wolsey, but the pronoun erects them into emblems of Envy. The tone that 'ye' creates in these passages is suggestive of the Preacher's "vanity of vanities".

If a constructive choice is being exercised in these Shakespearian examples (where people are beheld in a special way, the attitude to them is perceived to be different when they are addressed as 'ye') little motive seems to have guided Fletcher's frequent preference for this form in place of 'you', though clearly its occasional final unstressed position in the line contributes to the effect of pathos he so often attains. Throughout Fletcher's work, but especially that written after 1611, 'ye' occurs, and except that in a high proportion of these the speaker is being either (*a*) indignant or (*b*) pathetic, both highly typical Fletcherian attitudes, no principle guiding its selection seems clear. It is a lighter word than 'you', more quickly uttered and represents a vocal fronting. As such it consorts with the general temperament of his verse.

Consider the following where ineffectual indignation, self-pity, pathos are combined in a single speech to produce a highly characteristic result:

> She cannot dye, she must not dye; are those
> I plant my love upon but common livers?
> Their hours as others, told 'em? can they be ashes?
> Why do ye flatter a belief into me
> That I am all that is, the world's my creature,
> The Trees bring forth their fruits when I say Summer,
> The Wind that knows no limit but his wildness,
> At my command moves not a leaf; the Sea
> With his proud mountain waters envying Heaven,
> When I say still, run into Crystal mirrors,
> Can I do this and she dye? Why ye bubbles
> That with my least breath break, no more remembered;
> Ye moths that fly about my flame and perish,
> Ye golden canker-worms, that eat my honours,
> Living no longer than my spring of favour:
> Why do ye make me God that can do nothing?
> Is she not dead?
>
> (*Valentinian*, IV. i)

A Roman Emperor, worshipped as a god, is unable to prevent

the woman he loves from dying—and Fletcher is remembering some passages in *King Lear*. But unlike Lear, in his self-pity, how remote is Valentinian from a realization of the actuality of the human condition. Valentinian is pathetic, not tragic, and we hear the typical Fletcherian *tremulo* in his voice, a *tremulo* that subdues everything in the lines—the customary imagery, etc.— to itself. But if this is Fletcher's intention, and something he does often, he yet does it well. And if we substituted 'you' for the 'ye' this *tremulo* effect is largely destroyed, because there would be (i) a vocal lowering and retreat in the utterance, (ii) a consequent slowing-up of the speed with which the lines can be said, (iii) a shift of attention from the tremulous sound to the pictorial imagery, and (iv) the remote and generalizing meaning of 'ye' would go in favour of a more particularizing word. Valentinian would be speaking to someone instead of attitudinizing his grief. The speech would cease to be what it is—characteristic Fletcher—and become something less interesting—sub-Shakespeare.

Fletcher on his own, or in partnership with someone other than Beaumont, often sacrificed pronominal pointers to meaning in order to indulge his temperamental love for the 'dying fall'. For Fletcher the struggle was not the impossible one of enunciating the truth of an individual *thou-ness* (and every 'thou' is finally and desperately individual) but to entertain his audience. Hence the stress on the unique 'situation' rather than the unique person, and this it is that makes his verbs more important than his pronouns. Beaumont and Fletcher's work is, as they say, eminently Baroque: but to identify the Baroque in literature it is necessary to look not so much at the ornament of imagery (which is passively at the mercy of the verbs determining the situation) but at the Verbs. And these refuse to fix deeds, to define states of being which can be relied on for a duration beyond their naming, or to stay still.

Unlike Shakespeare's verbs (considered in the main) or Tourneur's, or Jonson's, or Webster's, Fletcher's are of the IF variety. But Fletcher was catering for an audience in a way these other dramatists never suffered themselves to do, and his verbial IF mechanics must be read in terms of an interpretation of that audience.

Of that audience Professor John F. Danby has written admirably.[1] It was an audience which needed phantasies not only to delude but also to nourish them. In the delusion lay the nourishment. (Beaumont and) Fletcher's plays spring from an *if*. Supposing, they say, we are in Rhodes (or Armenia, or Iberia, or Cordova, or Thessaly) and supposing that the king has a Divine Right (like the king in *The Maid's Tragedy*), and supposing that this king, on the strength of the absolute obedience owed him, commands of a subject a task which offends every other sanction, then. . . . Then what? It is for the satisfaction of the curiosity roused by this question, provoked in the first place by an unreal hypothesis, that Beaumont and Fletcher's plays exist.

The whole of a (Beaumont and) Fletcher play might be said to take place in a Subjunctive Mood. Adopting a phrase of Keats', "it begins and ends in pure speculation". Positing unreal conditions (*The Custom of the Country* is a notorious instance), a play goes on to find its solution within the same Mood in which it had its beginning.

So to exploit the appeal of Conditional Subjunctive as successfully as they did was an achievement which only two such alert, and even brilliant, minds could have done at that time. And this Conditional Subjunctive, having no referential communication with the Indicative—such as we find in Shakespeare's Final Plays—required special fluency for its dramatic habitation. Now one of the prices of this fluency was the lowering of barriers, between Pronouns—between 'thou' and 'you', and 'you' and 'ye'—with 'thou' and 'ye' ready to be called on only when the 'action' called for indignant pathos. Perhaps Beaumont had been conscious of such distinctions but, with his retirement from the stage, Fletcher lost the partner who might have checked his inclination to indulge his own—and his audience's—weakness by referring them to the distinctions perceived by an older generation.

4 SOME CONCLUSIONS

On Jonson's testimony most of Donne's profane love poems were written before the poet had completed his twenty-fifth

[1] *Poets on Fortune's Hill*, pp. 152 ff.

year. His poems of divine love were probably written in his middle or late-middle age, though of course there was some overlapping of the two groups of poems. They belong to a period later than *The Revenger's Tragedy*. This explains the order with which we have dealt with our writers.

From early Donne to Fletcher—over a period, that is, of some twenty-five to thirty years—we see in the poetry, lyric and dramatic, a variety of usage with respect to 'thou', 'you', 'ye'. Much of this variety must be attributed to the individual natures of the poets and their poetry. Much must also be attributed to the difference between lyric and drama. Shakespeare, in the *Sonnets*, and Donne, in the poems we have considered, are addressing an audience of one; while Tourneur, Shakespeare in his plays, and Beaumont and Fletcher are writing in what Mr. Eliot has termed 'the third voice' where the poet is "inventing speech in which imaginary characters address each other".[1] Though even this requires extensive qualification: for instance, it might be truer to say that Shakespeare of the *Sonnets* and Donne of *Songs and Sonets* are *assuming* themselves to be addressing an audience of one; that Donne more directly addresses, that Shakespeare (rather) is overheard addressing; that Donne more boldly presumes to know the wishes and feelings of the one he addresses, and so can use 'we' with a confidence we do not find in Shakespeare; that Donne speaks as much *for* himself as *to* another, etc.

But when allowances have been made for the different *genres* of poetry in which they wrote, and the different natures of the poets and their poetry, the changes—to which we have drawn attention—point to certain conclusions.

But let us recollect our findings.

Tourneur, in some key passages of *The Revenger's Tragedy*, clearly distinguishes between 'thou' and 'you'. Not of course that 'thou' has but a single meaning for him, and 'you' another single, though distinct, meaning. It would be absurd to suggest as much. Consider, for example, that today we refer to those in our company, singular or plural, by the common word 'you'. And every time we use the word it has a different meaning. We love, hate, respect, despise or are emotionally indifferent towards those to whom we say 'you'. Neither is our feeling, or

[1] *The Three Voices of Poetry*, p. 4.

attitude, to any one of them strictly constant. More than any other Part of Speech the Personal Pronouns—since their usage implies not one but two variables, human beings and their relationships—are relative in their meaning.

What we intend, then, is that, for Tourneur, 'thou' *covered one area of meaning* and 'you', by contrast, *served the multiplicity of occasions for the indication of individuals*. 'Thou' stood for the skull and the whole collection of attitudes to Death—and so to worldly life—which the Middle Ages had developed. The skull was a symbol, and a symbol was addressed as 'Thou'.

Yet we have chosen but one example. Not only the collective attitudes to Death, but the collective attitudes towards any other area of knowledge or emotion (and this includes God) providing that it had bred a symbol, or become personalized, or taken on a proper name, was worthy of being addressed as 'Thou'. Any such 'Thou' could be regarded with wonder, dread, reverence, awe, admiration or other religious emotion. The reality of the emotions, deriving from long tradition, which such a 'Thou' aroused, invests a 'Thou' in the verse of Tourneur with a force that is altogether absent in the 'thou', as used towards some classical mythological figure, or personalized abstraction, in, say, eighteenth-century pastoral verse. In Tourneur, 'Thou' has much meaning, in the eighteenth century little.

Now, in Tourneur, 'you' could be put beside 'thou' to generate a sense of friction. One and the same person-thing—the skull—can be addressed as 'Thou' and 'you'. Alternately, but not as simple alternatives. 'Thou' and 'you' were not synonyms. 'You' had its multiple individual applications; 'thou' its consistency. In moving from one term to another, in setting one approach against another, Tourneur could broach discoveries startling and effective. All we have done is to point an instance that could be multiplied; and these instances would further illustrate the truth that in *The Revenger's Tragedy* 'Thou' and 'you' were functionally separate, and that he used the words as effective instruments in his verse.

In the two groups of Donne's poems we see—partly because, we remind ourselves, he wrote lyrics—'thou' has a very great but different significance. In *Songs and Sonets*, 'thou' does not stand for a traditional collection of attitudes towards an area of knowledge or a feeling, but is an implement for designating an otherwise un-nameable personal essence. 'Thou', in Donne, is not an inclusive but a singularizing word, a concentrating means of address to the *haecceitas* of the woman he loved or with the uniqueness of God. Therefore, in the love poems of Donne, profane or sacred, 'thou' has a central place in the meaning. The word 'thou' occurs in a poem, and the rest of the poem attempts definition or analysis of that word 'thou'. In no other poet does the word mean so much. He developed it for his own specific needs, and no succeeding poet—not even among his metaphysical followers—was able to refine on its meaning in Donne's terms, or even in their own. The word deteriorated and this is Donne's responsibility. In using, and exploring, the word so intensively in his own way, he reduced its efficiency for fulfilling those earlier purposes to which his own had run counter. He enfeebled it for those who would use it for purposes related to those of the author of *The Revenger's Tragedy*—as an inclusive.

In Fletcher the word has neither the virtue of the 'Thou' of *The Revenger's Tragedy* nor the contrasting excellence of the 'thou' of *Songs and Sonets*. Some distinction between 'thou' and 'you' exists, and when Beaumont, perhaps, is at hand, the two words are used for different purposes. Beaumont might be remembering their difference of meaning and trying to put that memory to effect. But with Fletcher, working alone, we mainly see that 'thou' and 'you' are forms whose usage is to be regulated by social etiquette.

V The Metaphysicals' Craft of
the Verb

I PRELIMINARY

THE plays of Fletcher beginning with a 'let us suppose . . .
this', or 'assuming that . . .', arouse a curiosity whose satisfaction is delayed as long as possible. When the satisfaction
comes it is seen to be even less related to what we recognize as
actuality than was the initial curiosity. Fletcher's plays are contained by the Subjunctive and the manœuvring that takes place
is a manœuvring of tenses within that Mood. In contrast to this
art of Fletcher, many of the most admired, yet elaborate *lyrics*,
of his own generation, or of the generation following, depend
for their success on a studied interplay between Moods. Dual-
moded, they achieve whatever they do achieve from a strategy,
even sportiveness, of mind which starting with a 'let us suppose',
a subjunctive posture, then takes a jump to find an end, or solution, in the Indicative. Thus their Verb-machinery works
counter to that of Shakespeare in his last plays. More important,
the Verb-machinery of the more admired metaphysical poems
works oppositely to the Verb-machinery of poems of the nineteenth century. The admiration bestowed by the 1930's on the
metaphysicals was—so far as Poetic Grammar is concerned—
promoted by the, perhaps largely unconscious, discovery that
these poets had begun with the Subjunctive to end with the
Indicative instead of *vice versa*.

We will illustrate this by reference to two famous and, in
their way, excellent poems. Doing this, we should remember
that we are not concerned with any mere grammatical quibble

nor with any sort of ingenuity for its own sake. Rather, we should remember that the formal division of an English verb's conjugation into Moods reflects a profound division of being as schematized by the human mind but known to the soul.[1]

To instance this, let us take the verb that all people are—or should be—most concerned with: to love. We insert the qualification as a reminder that many transfer their interest, when a stage of life is reached from *to love* to *to have* or *to get*: acquisitiveness supplanting lust. Now on one side of the conjugation of the verb to love is the Indicative. And the Indicative expresses facts or actualities occurring in Time which are conveyed by Tense. Thus, for example: I love; thou wilt love; he was loving *or* used to love; we loved *or* we have loved; you will have loved; they had loved. Hence, if one is sure of the facts, one is also sure of instruments for expressing them—whether the love exists, once certainly existed, or did so in a still remoter past, or whether it will exist in a time to come. Yet as literature —if not our own lives—reveals, actual accomplishments in this verb's indicative do not suffice or contain desire, and the excess —whether of wish or regret—requires, for its expression, that other Mood of the Subjunctive. The door of desire is hinged and has another side to the one we see when enclosed in our room. Or to move from the image of the leaf of the door to the leaves of books: in our Grammar books there is the page either facing the Indicative, or on the other side of the same leaf on which the Indicative is printed, which orders into Tenses not the facts of, but the possibilities of, desire. Now the life of desire in this realm of the Subjunctive is unacted and unsatisfied (turn the leaves as we may), and yet this life is as real as the life in the indicative world of actuality, an equality of status suggested by the Continental grammarians' term: (not *Sub-* but) *Con*junctive Mood. But not only is there perpetual conflict between the life of fact and the life of desire, but within the subjunctive realm itself there can be continual and great tension. For the subjunctive world of wish, or desire, is also the world of moral oughts. Whereas the indicative world is the concern of the scientist, the subjunctive realm is the concern of the poet and the moralist,

[1] I am aware that what is known as the Subjunctive Mood in Latin is the result of a conflation of *two* yet older Moods: an old Subjunctive expressing will (and futurity) and an old Optative expressing desire (and futurity).

and within this realm the claims of poet and moralist custom-arily conflict.

The two poems we are about to consider must be appre-hended as poems recognizing the existence of opposed Moods. It is from a study of the Verb Forms in the poems that an appreciation of their meaning is best secured and, in each case, the meaning determines their structure.

2 'TO HIS COY MISTRESS': ARGUMENT BY MOOD

A total of forty-six lines, in three paragraphs, go to make up Marvell's *To his Coy Mistress*. Of these forty-six lines the first paragraph claims as many as twenty. (The second has twelve, the third fourteen.) Now it should be understood that the whole of this first paragraph—with the exception of the nineteenth line, which states a fact, namely:

> For Lady you deserve this State;[1]

—is a deliberate exercise within the limits of the subjunctive. Within the limits? But that is a paradox, because in the sub-junctive realms, unlike the indicative world which is inexorably limited by dimensions of time and space, there are no limits. This indeed is what the poem says.

The poem begins:

> Had we but World enough, and Time . . .

'Supposing we were freed from the laws of time and space. . . .' It is 'supposing' for, of course, Marvell knows very well—only too well—that he and his mistress are not free. Starting with the Conditional "Had we" (and we notice that by the simple exchange of the natural-sounding order—'we had' —for one requiring a strong emphasis on the first element, a final difference is effected between a statement of a past *fact* and a desired situation which can *never* be arrived at), there is an extended disporting in the Subjunctive—the impossible pos-sible. Yet Marvell is not doing as Romantic poets, lovers and lunatics do: deluding himself that subjunctive *is* indicative. Remembering the stress on his first word, Marvell is playing a game, and knows that he is playing a game. He knows, and we

[1] Quotations are from the edition of H. M. Margoliouth.

know, that this play at 'choosing within the subjunctive' is to be
set against a knowledge of unalterable indicatives, even though
a statement of that knowledge is to be deliberately withheld
until the opening of the second paragraph with its famous
shock:

> But at my back I alwaies hear
> Times winged Charriot . . .

followed by a series of notes on the checks to will imposed by
death and the laws of space. Marvell is not going to assert
subjunctive truth as did Shakespeare in his Final Plays; rather
he is going to expose the folly of dwelling in hope and the
consequent need for immediate action.

But to watch him at his game. Granting the initial premise,
then what *would* 'we' do? he asks. Yet it is not quite that, for
there is no 'we'—no wit-ness[1]—so long as coyness puts space
between them; there is no 'we' until their two strengths and
sweetnesses are in "one Ball"; rather it is a question of what "I
would" and "you should" do:

> Thou by the *Indian Ganges* side
> Should'st Rubies find: I by the Tide
> Of *Humber* would complain. I would
> Love you ten years before the Flood:
> And you should if you please refuse
> Till the Conversion of the *Jews*.

So it is at the beginning of their pretended enfranchisement
from the laws of time and space. But the pretended situation
develops. He has a lover's duties ('should's' or 'ought's') as well
as a lover's desires ('would's'), and he ought to pay the tribute,
in measure of time, that her beauty deserves:

> An hundred years should go to praise
> Thine Eyes, and on thy Forehead Gaze.
> Two hundred to adore each Breast:
> But thirty thousand to the rest.

(Here, it will be noticed, that as his gaze travels down her
naked length, the tribute owed to her parts, and expressed by
measures of time, naturally increases!)

Thus, supposing what is impossible to be possible, Marvell

[1] For 'wit'-ness, see above, p. 88.

plays within the one Mood that does allow freedom of play. The lover has a persistency of desire (he 'would') where the will is free; his mistress has persistency of choice (she 'should—if she pleases'). It might seem that the paragraph is a product of fancy which, as Coleridge tells us:

> . . . is indeed no other than a mode of memory emancipated from the order of time and space; while it is blended with, and modified by that empirical phenomenon of the will, which we express by the word Choice.[1]

But I do not here imply—though Coleridge does—any inferiority of fancy with respect to any other power. The fancy of the first paragraph of *To his Coy Mistress* is necessary to the structure of argument of the whole poem.

Desiring and choosing are both subjunctive activities and, being independent of the indicative laws of space, partake of heaven—with this difference: in heaven (who knows!) the desiring and choosing of one solitary will attains satisfaction, and so end; but, on earth, two wills are necessary; two choices must coincide: the lover's *and* his mistress's. Here, on earth, within the freedom of the subjunctive, he is prepared to await, for as long as *she* chooses, the time (desire demanding satisfaction, even the Subjunctive has its, albeit ghostly, Future[2]) when he and she will be in "one Ball". But:

> . . . at my back I alwaies hear
> Times winged Charriot hurrying near:
> And yonder all before us lye
> Desarts of vast *Eternity*.

Though in the first paragraph Marvell had played the fancy of pretended freedom from the laws of time and space, *supposing* himself and his mistress to have an eternity in which to dally, yet he reminds her and us that they will have "desarts" of that soon. That "vast Eternity" is an indicative certainty and the second paragraph is one of indicative reminders. Indicatively we are bound by time and space for a few years. After that death. And, whatever death is, it will certainly not bring one thing: the opportunity for their bodies to get into "one Ball". But that opportunity certainly exists *now*—in the Indicative. It will, with equal certainty, not exist—even the most orthodox

---

[1] *Biographia Literaria*, chapter XIII. [2] See pp. 7, 8, above.

will be constrained to admit this—in the "Desarts of vast
Eternity", or at most—if we can allow the indicative and
temporal into the context—not until the Resurrection, and then
dubitably. And, even if indubitably, then differently because
the bodies will be of a different kind.

Thus, placed in the Indicative, the second paragraph is
properly a catalogue of reminders of the conditions on the
recognition of which the conjugation of the Indicative Mood is
precisely constructed. The conditions are of time and space:

> Thy Beauty shall no more be found;
> Nor, in thy marble Vault, shall sound
> My ecchoing Song: then Worms shall try. . . .

The insistency of the auxiliary 'shall' tells us that though the
whole of the second paragraph is cast into one Mood—*contra*
that Mood of the first paragraph—yet the focus is, in fact,
narrower still than that. Except for the generally true statements of its last two lines, it is cast into a single Tense of that
Mood—the Future. *Future* facts or certainties are stated. In the
context of their paragraph they have their powerful effect, less
in themselves than because they occur in a paragraph that is of
verbial purity. The facts derive their power from the paragraph
and the paragraph derives its power because, engineered all in
one Tense and Mood, it follows the first paragraph which is
engineered purely in another Mood. Yet it is not so much that
the two paragraphs conflict, as that they contrast. For, in
seeking *to enjoy* (an activity, demanding a verb) his Mistress
Marvell discovers two prospects to her: one pretending to offer
gratification in the end—but this is known to be illusory; the
other of a state, soon to be reached, where there can be no
enjoyment of anything. Each prospect is governed by a Verb
Form; the first by a form where Time is evaded, the other by a
form where Time determines. One prospect is unreal, the other
real and barren. Neither offers a course of action within the
terms of the verb *to enjoy*. This reduces the hope of action to one
Tense—the Present.

As the subjunctive 'would's and 'should's ruled the first
paragraph; and as the auxiliary 'shall', denoting future
certainty, ruled the second paragraph; so does the adverb of

time 'now' followed by a First Person plural 'let us' (for *to enjoy* love, the choice must be mutual) of the Imperative Mood, rule the last paragraph:

> Now therefore, while the youthful hew
>
> . . . .
>
> Now let us sport us while we may:
> And now, like am'rous birds of prey,
> Rather at once our Time devour,
> Than languish in his slow-chapt pow'r.
> Let us roll. . . .

In a frame of the Imperative, the Mood not of present enjoyment but of invitation to present enjoyment, the present action unreally exists. Unreally, for if the poet's "strength" and his mistress's "sweetness" were actually rolled up "into one Ball" there would be no need to plead for that state or action. The meaning of the Verb, and not the word for it, would be a present experienced. Nor—then—would any of the poem be necessary. The point of arguing this is that the last two lines of the paragraph (which like its predecessors is in a different tense from the rest of the unit which it concludes) *suggest* that a translation from the Imperative to the Present Indicative had been made. In fact, of course, the poet is anticipating.

We have said enough, I think, to show that the structure of *To his Coy Mistress* is rigorously determined by its Verb Forms. It is a poem in three sections in three contrasting Tenses and Moods, each section, having adopted its chosen Tense or Mood, remaining pure in its choice. It is this dominance of the Verbs, and Marvell's respect for the laws of time and space—the Personal Pronouns being at the mercy of the nouns of which they are the subject or complement—and with the freedom of choice restricted to freedom within these laws—which this dominance implies, that makes the poem so severely classical and gives it that "tough reasonableness" of which Mr. Eliot speaks.

As for the Pronouns. Like Donne's *Songs and Sonets*, *To his Coy Mistress* is an 'I' to 'thou' poem. The aim of the poem is that 'I' and 'thou' should become a 'we', that the 'thou' should consent to the 'I's' pleading so that this comes about. But Marvell is not, as Donne was, consistent. The Mistress is variously addressed as 'thou' or 'you'. No clear principle seems to govern the use of the two forms, beyond the nonce effect to be gained by one in place of the other. But it is apparent, of course, that the identity of Marvell's Coy Mistress is not apprehended as unique in the way that the identity of the woman Donne addresses is apprehended as unique in her 'thou-ness'.

We have said the poem is 'classical'. It is so also because its philosophy is pagan. In *To his Coy Mistress*, no more than in Catullus' "*Vivamus, mea Lesbia, atque amemus*", is it recognized that the doctrines of Christianity imply a modification of the conjugations; that its doctrines and beliefs, notably those of personal immortality and the resurrection of the body, altered previous conceptions of time, and of future time in particular. Moreover, Shakespeare, with or without the aid of those doctrines and beliefs, had altered the conjugation of the Future, and of other tenses, in his Final Plays. Yet that Christianity had intervened between Catullus and himself is ignored in Marvell's poem. *To his Coy Mistress* has the same view of the future as "*Vivamus, mea Lesbia, atque amemus*", and hence in its final paragraph makes the same entreaty as Catullus' poem as a whole. Yet, a generation or two earlier, Jonson had set his translation of Catullus' poem within the Christian terms of *Volpone*, as a lure certainly, but as a lure whose falsity was immediately to be perceived.

But that a stringent respect for Verbs as the basis of composition, and a deliberate manipulation of their Moods, is a mark of seventeenth-century metaphysical poetry—independent of whether the philosophy of the poet is pagan or Christian—is a claim which our next section will endeavour to support further.

3 'THE EXEQUY': RESOLUTION THROUGH TENSE

A structural dialogue between opposed, and yet complementary, Moods provides the dynamic of the chief most obviously Christian love poem of the period no less surely than it does of its chief most obviously pagan love poem.

It rested with Mr. Eliot to discover to us Henry King's *The Exequy* as a *great* poem. In *The Oxford Book of English Verse* it had appeared in a 'cut' version. That should hardly be possible now, for the adjective 'great' implies the indispensability of parts.

And we are right to consider it alongside *To his Coy Mistress*. Not only are they both love poems—of love, whose enjoyment is lost or unsatisfied—but they are both Time poems. Both writers find the life of love—that is, the positive expression of love—subject to Time and problematic. Therefore the solution of the problem in poetry is also to be achieved through first a contemplation and then a manipulation of Tense. And of Mood. Rejecting the timeless Mood, Marvell's poem proposes the solution as lying in the Present Tense. King's, rejecting hope in the Present and Future Indicative Tenses, proposes the solution as lying in the timeless. Yet the dialectic *method* is the same in both cases.

The tensal outline of *The Exequy* is wonderfully bold.

The first half of the poem, sixty out of a hundred and twenty lines, is a backward-looking action. King is spending his present time contemplating his past time. This is the verbial mechanism of regret. In his *now* he is engaged in the action of regret, which can be as firmly formularized by the sign ← as the opposite action of hope is expressed thus: →.[1] Yet meditate on the life of the past as he may, this is not life because it will not bring his wife back to life. In fact this ← looking of the mind is, in its way, an abuse of his indicative 'is-ness' and, as such, is as much a subjunctive activity as hope—more so: hope may be realized whereas regret cannot bring back, or redeem; not in this case, at least. Not that there need be "wonder", he says:

> if my time go thus
> Backward and most preposterous.[2]

But for all the great pathos of the excuse:

> . . . thy set
> This eve of blackness did beget,
> Who wast my day,

---

[1] These signs seem natural to me; but perhaps to those born into the Hebrew or Arabic, besides other, languages, and to left-handed Englishmen, they might seem more natural in reverse.

[2] *The Caroline Poets*, Vol. III, edited by George Saintsbury, p. 195.

he knows he is looking the wrong way in looking ←, and this is 'backward'. Moreover, in looking the wrong way, he is advancing in time 'arsy-versy', i.e. arse-foremost. For, to King, if not for us, 'preposterous' was no simple equivalent for 'outrageous' but carried the literal meaning of the Latin which he applies metaphorically. If King is being consciously funny (a more accurate word than 'witty' in this circumstance), then by this funniness he reminds us that he is in control in that he *knows* that being simply regretful is to look in the wrong direction, a perverse way of dealing with 'time', which therefore "lazily creeps about". Indeed, that this "preposterous" spending of time in the subjunctive of the gone past is to refuse to live, he admits when he says:

> For thee (lov'd clay)
> I languish out, not live, the day.

Yet in this state of regret he does more than merely look backward and proceed arsy-versy.[1] He subjunctively tampers with the past by playing games with—or in—a false future as in the next paragraph:

> I could allow thee, for a time,
> To darken me and my sad clime,
> Were it a month, a year, or ten,
> I would thy exile live till then;
> And all that space my mirth adjourn,
> So thou wouldst promise to return;
> And putting off thy ashy shroud,
> At length disperse this sorrow's cloud.

As in Marvell's first paragraph this is a deliberate Subjunctive 'let's pretend'. But the two poems agree on this: both will repudiate their opening Moods. Marvell's fantastic wishes to override the laws of time and King's equally fantastic reclamatory wishes (he is to call them "these empty hopes") are alike to be rejected as unreal.

[1] *The Exequy* is a very beautiful and very moving poem. To avoid misunderstandings it should be said that I am not blaming King even when he blames himself. It is a beautiful and moving poem because King confesses to behaving as a human being in a situation—that of the survivor of a marriage—which the majority of people must experience. No-one can do more than behave as a human being; the sin is in doing less than is expected of a human being.

For King acknowledges:

> 'twixt me and my soul's dear wish
> The earth now interposed is,

and that is indicative enough. Spade-fulls of earth now form (in time and space) a ponderable block between a real past, which is now but a retrospective subjunctive of desire, and his present is-ness of deprivation.

The straight realization of this fact, cutting across the pretence that his wife has gone away on a holiday, compels at length the modal change—from the comforting but deluding Subjunctive to the Indicative. There is first the Present:

> the longest date
> Too narrow is to calculate
> These empty hopes.

And this realization leads to another, and in another tense, in the Future:

> never shall I
> Be so much blest as to descry
> A glimpse of thee, till that day come,
> Which shall the earth to cinders doom,
> And a fierce fever must calcine
> The body of this world, like thine,
> My Little World! That fit of fire
> Once off, our bodies shall aspire
> To our souls' bliss . . .

—lines which state not the "empty hopes" of the Subjunctive but real and dreadful future facts. As Mr. Eliot has said, this is a poem which could have been written in no period other than its own. The doctrines of Christianity, including that of a Last Day and a Bodily Resurrection of the dead, are 'for King' facts and as such require the unequivocal firmness of the Indicative. It is not a matter of subjunctive hope but of indicative truth that the bodies of his wife and himself will rise to invest their souls so that they will see each other in the flesh:

> . . . we shall rise,
> And view ourselves with clearer eyes
> In that calm region, where no night
> Can hide us from each other's sight.

This *will* come about in time, on which tense is constructed but, having come to pass, there will be no more tense.

It should also be noted that up to this point, the poem has
been a lament of an 'I' for a lost 'thou'. It has been an 'I' to
'thou' or 'thee' poem, like—in this respect—Marvell's *To his
Coy Mistress*. The 'I' and the 'thou' of King's poem have been,
or are, separated by time and space. With this consummation of
longing and desire—for which the annihilation of time and
space, confidently foreseen, is the condition—the Pronoun of
the First Person plural, the 'we' and 'us' of the quotation, make
their first and only appearance. This reveals the nature of the
poem. King's inability to use the Pronoun 'we' with Present
Indicative truth is the *raison d'être* of the lament. The point at
which he realizes that he will be able to use the word in the
future—though only at a position in the future when the word
'future' ceases to have meaning (the timeless Subjunctive of
desire gained, but gained in Indicative actuality) is the turning-
point of the poem. With his sights laid on this 'we' he ceases to
lament and instead becomes "content" that "Heaven's will"
has divided them for the duration of all time; becomes ready,
even, to make an elaborate and excellent joke:

> Meantime, thou hast her, Earth; much good
> May my harm do thee . . .

—yet the Earth had better look out! what she has is "lent" not
given, and each "grain and atom" of his wife's "dust" must be
yielded back when she (and the poet with her) is re-assembled
in the flesh at the Resurrection. Thus he arrives at the stage of
contemplation when she is not merely not dead but sleeping,
yet sleeping in a special kind of bed:

> So close the ground, and 'bout her shade
> Black curtains draw;—my Bride is laid.
>
> Sleep on, my Love, in thy cold bed,
> Never to be disquieted!

Henceforth, in the poem, King is not spending his time 'pre-
posterously' or 'arsy-versy'. His gaze is directed forward: he is
'looking forward', as the idiom has it, into the Future Indicative,
to the occasion when time will

> Marry my body to that dust
> It so much loves; and fill the room
> My heart keeps empty in thy tomb.

Moreover, in 'looking forward' he becomes warm in the anticipation, and though he cannot finish the journey ("Through which to *Thee* I swiftly glide") soon enough, yet the pace of the verse quickens as the ardour of his imagination intensifies:

> But heark! My pulse, like a soft drum,
> Beats my approach, tells *Thee* I come;
> And slow howe'er my marches be,
> I shall at last sit down by *Thee*.

He is spending his time reversely to the way he began. He is now living and living *for* a dissolution which will precede a reunion in the flesh.

4 REFLECTIONS

To his Coy Mistress and *The Exequy* are both fine poems and, though having much in common, are yet complementary to each other. Both are long enough to permit changes of Tense and transitions of Mood. But the problem confronting Marvell and King—how to overcome impediments imposed by time and space so as to enjoy union with a loved person—compels just such changes and transitions in the attempt to find its solution; for no *lasting* solution to any problem can be reached within the terms of one Tense or even one Mood. Both their external length and their internal structure, which are created by these Tense-changes and Mood-transitions, absolutely prevent these poems being considered as lyrics. A lyric, e.g. King's "Tell me no more how fair she is", is not only a short poem meant to be sung but it is a poem cast in one Mood and Tense, and though it may pose a problem it does not attempt to solve it.

Moreover, because of their attempt to solve a problem, Marvell's *Coy Mistress* and King's *Exequy* are not 'strophic' but 'paragraph' poems. The unevenness in the lengths of their paragraphs—more marked in King's case than in Marvell's for the reason that the former's poem is more original and more personally felt by the author while Marvell's plea '*carpe diem*' follows a traditional formula of argument over whose stages, in the course of the ages, a semi-strophic regularity has been imposed—follows from this tensal and modal gear-changing.

Marvell's poem is, then, the more impersonal. Though it is

not necessarily the worse for that, it explains the apparent haphazardness in his use of 'thou' and 'you', to which we have referred above. Mr. F. W. Bateson who privately reports to me that he had once attempted to see whether Marvell, in this poem, was guided by any principle confesses that it seemed that Marvell considered the words as mere synonyms. To Marvell it was the mutual enjoyment he had with the girl, not her identity, that mattered. But King, who consistently uses 'thou', certainly sensed the unique 'thou'-ness of his wife. And his poem was possibly written earlier than Marvell's. In thought and structure of sensibility it is in some respect a more conservative poem than Marvell's.

Judging by the verbial changes which structure these poems, we see that the breath-unit of the indicative is comparatively short. We say the truth and end, but we hope or regret in larger spirals.

Marvell and King attempt to solve their problem with the aid of traditional philosophies. Marvell's philosophy is the more venerable. While King's had a mere thirteen hundred years' or so history, Marvell's was respectable in the sun-battened yards of the tenements of Rome centuries before Augustine of Canterbury was born. What is remarkable, however, is Marvell's well-nigh[1] total exclusion of Christianity from his poem and from the reader's mind while he is actually reading the poem. So to render us momentarily unaware that Christian philosophy had ever intervened in time between himself and the Rome of Catullus is an extraordinary success of art. But while both poets attempt to reach a solution to a problem through the aid of a philosophy, it must be admitted that while King found a solution—the only solution—satisfactory, at least, to himself, Marvell's solution depends, even at his poem's conclusion, on the consent of the girl's will to his Imperative invitation.

Nevertheless, both poems exercise the same mechanics of the Verb. In effecting a transition from an initial Subjunctive to an Indicative they illustrate a procedure of the seventeenth-century mind. It is this procedure, more than anything else, which distinguishes the Metaphysicals from the Romantics. In Keats or Shelley the procedure is the opposite one of a movement from

[1] For there is a reference to the conversion of the Jews!

a hated Indicative to a Subjunctive and the discovery that it is this Subjunctive which is only 'real'. Instead of the articles of common belief being prescriptive of hope, the substance of individual hope becomes accessible to belief.

VI *Limited Verb and Pronoun*

I PRELIMINARY

THIS is not a chapter I shall enjoy. I enjoy most writing about those poems I enjoy most. It is not enjoyable to perform the negative office of pointing to deficiencies in poems as the miserable excuse for one's relative lack of enjoyment. Nor, generally, does such a procedure do any good. As a general rule, if one does not enjoy vastly, better leave alone to those who do; for they can see more than oneself by reason of their superior enjoyment. Yet it is necessary to deal next with three poets—in what may seem an unfriendly way—though they are, indeed, great poets, happily able to endure any kind of criticism with ease. Moreover the criticism is directed less at them than at the kinds of 'situation' in which they wrote—situations which imply too *restricted* a conception of the quality, variety and range of being of every single man or women whether living today or (even) in their own times. As a result the Grammar of these poets is restricted. Though they can be enjoyed (all have given me delight and I hope I am not being too ungrateful) for the Grammar they do, in fact, manage to encompass and affirm, and (also) for all sorts of other virtues (which are not our present concern), yet it is their limitations—their actual omissions of certain inflexions in the play of their poetry—that compel me to treat, however briefly, of them here as negative examples or *exempla horrenda*. I am merely concerned here with what Pope, Crabbe and part of Wordsworth do *not* possess in the way of inflexions, with the results of this want on their poetry, and with the inferences which we can consequently draw with respect to the human settings in which they wrote. I am not concerned here with the specific wonders which each of these poets individually achieved—wonders which we cannot afford to reject, and which are, in truth, denied to other poets (let them possess, I am almost tempted to add, whatever inflexions one—or they themselves—will!).

2 POPE AND THE VERB SIMPLE

Hitherto, in these pages, 'Tense' and 'Mood' have referred either to particular verbial inflexions occurring within a poem (in which case they can be more or less structural—the internal tenses and moods of *To his Coy Mistress* and *The Exequy*, for example, are highly structural, while the fact that changes of Tense and Mood occur in the lines of some other piece of verse might be of little significance for either the poem or the reader at all) or to the Tense or Mood *of* the poem. Here the poem has a sort of circumscribing Verb deriving from the poem's total components, among which of course must be reckoned the internal verbs and including, sometimes, as in *Macbeth*, the substance of the plot.

Now eighteenth-century verse as a whole, whether satirical, moral, reflective or narrative, tends to be verse of a single Tense and Mood. That Mood is Indicative, which is what one might expect of verse aimed primarily at making statements. But it is Indicative for other reasons as well: because of the *way* the verse addresses its audience or readers; because of the nature of that audience so addressed; because of the eighteenth century's conceptions of time and space. Moreover, within the Indicative a single, or at least a standard, Tense is preferred. The poet is concerned to state existing facts. What the poet and his audience does not know (and what they know they know in common and know in advance of the poem being written) either scarcely exists or is assumed not to exist. The life of *possibility* is hardly recognized.

Such is this Indicative and, largely, single Tense, poetry. It is not a question of maintaining that all the Verbs occurring in all eighteenth-century verse are in the Present or Past Perfect Indicative. That would, of course, be an absurd exaggeration easy to confute. Rather it is a question of realizing that the mass of eighteenth-century verse, if only because of its disinclination to entertain possibility, is both bounded and sustained by the Verbs in the Indicative Mood—though it does follow from this that among the internal Verbs (as a detailed study of passages of verse would reveal) the proportion of those in the Indicative is overwhelmingly high. But they dominate and they domineer. Subjunctive forms of course appear, though comparatively rarely, and when they do appear they do not have that intensively modifying or transforming effect on plain statement that they do in verse of other periods. The realm to which they belong is neglected or poorly esteemed, and being regarded as 'outside the pale' of a known reality is not only subordinate in importance (if not actually condemned) but is permitted little or no conversation with the Indicative. The Subjunctive is minor, suspected, and kept separate.

What we said of the Verbs of eighteenth-century verse in general applies, naturally enough, to Pope in particular. We illustrate this by quotations from *The Moral Essays*, although in truth it is of little importance from whichever part of his works we quote for, though his work steadily gains in mastery (within the terms it chose after *The Rape of the Lock*) in the course of its writer's career, it is throughout consistent in kind. The block is of one piece no matter where we chip:

> Nothing so true as what you once let fall,
> "Most Women have no Characters at all."
> Matter too soft a lasting mark to bear,
> And best distinguish'd by black, brown, or fair. . . .[1]

or:

> See how the World its Veterans rewards!
> A Youth of Frolics, an old Age of Cards;
> Fair to no purpose, artful to no end,
> Young without Lovers, old without a Friend;
> A Fop their Passion, but their Prize a Sot,
> Alive, ridiculous, and dead, forgot![2]

Here are admirable and quite representative bits of Pope at his best; though that it is possible to remove bits without inflicting mortal damage on the poem from which they are removed, or on the bits themselves, becomes in itself a basis for criticism. What an Epistle of Pope loses, if a piece is excided, is at most a vital link in the intellectual chain of argument: but

[1] *Moral Essays*, Epistle II, 1-4.   [2] *Ibid.*, 243-8.

remove a passage from *The Pardoner's Tale* and, leisurely or expansive as Chaucer may seem to be, not only is a step in the narrative missing but much extra-intellectual, or specifically poetic, cross-reference with the rest of the poem. And this distinction between the poetry of Pope and Chaucer in itself points to the different function of the Verb in the work of the two poets, which in turn reflects their different conceptions of time, possibility and action.

In the passages from Pope the Verbs have only local application. Though they perform their logical and syntactical purpose with a marvellous efficiency, having served that immediate purpose they do not act on the Verbs of other passages, or on passages as a whole, whether adjacent or far distant. Having served their immediate purpose their energy expires.

In our quotations the Verbs have this limited operation and it is this that gives such poetry of statement a curious flatness. But, equally, the Verbs have this limited operation, resulting in this flatness, because they all belong to the Indicative.

It might be replied that there is at least a variety of Tense, and that, for instance,

> Nothing so true as what you once let fall,
> "Most Women have no Characters at all",

sets an eternally present truth against a past opinion (and the occasion when it was uttered). But despite the lines' assurance, they probably pass off not a truth but a falsehood—as almost any 'opinion' is a falsehood when it is appealed to outside the temporary circumstances in which it was delivered. This particular 'opinion' may have had some life in its original setting, some power to convince at the moment it was delivered. But like other generalizings it does not bear later examination for then its frailty is exposed. Only the superficial truth of an opinion can survive and that is all that survives here.

If the opinion on women had been more than opinion—a perception, even a frenzied and distorted one, like, e.g., Lear's "Downe from the waste they are Centaures . . ." etc., then its recollection and placing beside Pope's immediate present might have had some gnomic authority. But an opinion is not a perception; and this leads us to another realization.

As the truth of an opinion, like the interest of a piece of news, is temporary, so Pope's poetry is true only of the age and society in which it was composed. As the second quotation shows there is an exclusion of all beyond the actuality of Pope's own time. Not only does little or nothing exist in the poetry, outside that which can be communicated by the Indicative, but there is little or nothing that cannot be observed in the Present—with an occasional reference to an immediate Past or near Future within that Mood. This exclusion of a past of various stages of temporal remoteness in either direction, no less than the exclusion of the subjunctival, ensures the flatness of Pope's verse. Pope's interests are local and his temporal focus is confined. To apply Tennyson, his characters have "Lives that lie/Foreshorten'd in the tract of time."

Responsibility for this state of affairs must be attributed, in part, to Pope's age no less than to Pope: its lack of veneration for the past, its satisfaction with its own time and plan. Pope's Verbs are one other aspect of Newtonian physics.

Finally, much of the sheer dullness of the part that the Verb is called on to play in Pope's poetry must also be attributed to eighteenth-century theories of the poet's job and to the structure of society which such theories assumed. According to such theories, Pope's job was not to *discover* (for himself or for others, for others through himself) but to *tell*. He was to instruct them in what they and he already knew. His audience—enviably large beside the expectancies of even the most widely-read of modern poets—was the one which had the active monopoly of political power and literary interests. Pope became one with his audience by virtue of his tremendous talent. As a member of this society he could either speak *for* it, or *to* it under the collective 'you', either explicitly or implicitly. He chose, mainly, 'you'. This is poetry of the Second Voice as Mr. Eliot has told us, but the relations which it presumes between the author and his audience enforce a severe limitation on the Verb which is the chief organ for expressing action and hence, because of that, of relations between persons.

Yet, when all has been said and done, Pope remains the author of the most brilliant—and, because so brilliant, almost the most beautiful of all couplets in English:

On her white breast a sparkling cross she wore,
Which Jews might kiss, and Infidels adore.[1]

[1] *The Rape of the Lock*, Canto II, 7–8.

The brilliance and beauty result from the play of the two Subjunctive Verbs in the second line *against* the Indicative of the first line. But the effect could not have been achieved but for the indicative limits which Jew and Turk 'might' transgress —limits assumed by Pope to be final.

3   CRABBE: THE SINGLE MOOD OF MORAL NARRATIVE

Crabbe's tales are moral tales. But the tale in verse which intends simply to *illustrate* a moral is, as poetry, limited if it succeeds in its intention; it will not extend human consciousness by adding to it a hitherto undiscovered domain. One remembers Coleridge's reply to Mrs. Barbauld when she complained that *The Ancient Mariner* had too little moral. Coleridge said he feared that his poem, on the contrary, had too much moral. He was surely right. The valedictory stanzas urging the duty of kindness to animals tend to make readers say that this is what *The Ancient Mariner* means, that this is its moral. But the poem finds out and says far more than this, and so it was perhaps a mistake of Coleridge's to write those concluding stanzas. His poem had explored what hitherto had been unknown. The reader is then invited to subscribe to what would serve as an admirable R.S.P.C.A. motto. There is nothing wrong in this if it is realized that the motto does not summarize the experience the poem offers and is no equivalent, expressed in moral terms, of that experience.

Yet Crabbe deserves great admiration for making the poet a story-teller once more. Worsted is stronger than silk and Crabbe's verse is stronger than Pope's. Byron said he was "Nature's sternest painter, yet the best". We can still agree, but only provided that we take as limited a view of truth as Crabbe himself does. Truth, for Crabbe, was that which was known or could be determined. It was the truth of actuality. To Crabbe man, woman or child can be known—known enough to be condemned—by their deeds and words. They are finite beings and can be placed in moral categories—which categories are conceived of in Indicative terms. Crabbe's truth is not speculative. Yet he has the virtue of his defect and his meticulous observation and rendering of the tangible details of landscape is as much part of his service to truth, as he saw it, as his account of human conduct. He wrote constantly of what was constant.

He was certainly constant in his performance. If there is no development during his career neither is there deterioration. As he was in *The Village* so he still is in *Tales of a Hall*—still recounting anecdotes of drunkards, sluggards, bullies, loose women, swindlers and poachers and always with a strong sour ease and often with a pungent confidence. These anecdotes are morally useful: they show the bad ends of bad people. We are warned by their example. The comparatively few tales of people of virtue serve a similar purpose: we are made to admire, if not imitate, the thrifty, the industrious, the sober and the honest. If we follow their example we shall earn rewards.

Crabbe's morality is, of course, grimly Protestant. Idleness, penury and dirt are, to him, sins. Drink is frowned on. Gaiety is frivolity. To be idle is to be poor, and—with a few signal exceptions of those who are poor through no fault of their own (e.g. an aged widow) and yet remain honest and content—those who are poor, steal.

Now this narrow morality, with its too few and self-evident precepts, is itself contributory to Crabbe's poetic practice of drawing on only half of the total resources of any one Verb. Within the orbit of his morality what bad people have done is so final that what they might have done instead does not exist. Their indicative acts *are*, or *were*, but their subjunctive realms never existed. Nor does any Subjunctive exist. What those people, whose names are in the parish register or in the gaol delivery list, could, should or might have done, or had desired to do (and may yet succeed in doing in the houses of the dead), as opposed to their indicative actions, is not included within the scope of Crabbe's verbs. A man is what he does, and that is sufficient. In Crabbe, as in Pope, knowledge is finite; but in Crabbe there is also a finitude of conduct. All conduct is here moral conduct and the reaches of ill-conduct are known. That evil things are done by individuals as alternatives to good acts, which their condition prevents them from carrying out, is not known to Crabbe. Moral alternatives exist but they only exist independent of a particular man's condition. This is to shut down on a belief in the subjunctive as the perpetual alternative existing for everyone and tends to an avoidance of the linguistic means of its communication—namely the Subjunctive Mood.

Crabbe points a moral by *remembering*. To illustrate the moral that honesty is the best policy "here is this tale . . .", he says. Hard upon this are related the ill-deeds of a thieving rogue who was at last deservedly punished. Now, in narrating these deeds, Crabbe, the craftsman, may slide to direct speech or to the historic present. But the tense of direct speech is set in the past of a severe and prudent memory. Crabbe is not like Chaucer (cf. *The Pardoner's Tale*) who tells of the former acts of dead men which still operate in the context of the living. Crabbe's actions were perfected in the past. The tense of his memory is that of the Past Perfect. Hence we are researching in the closed files of the Police Court and not, as with Chaucer, overhearing the secrets of a Confessional for ever in session.

But Crabbe, if he sees single, sees straight. Moreover, unlike his predecessors, he did not know that we know so little; he was too late, as well as too early, to know that we are dreams as well as actors, and that "what you do not know is the only thing you know".[1] Crabbe is like those parents who condemn the actions of their children because they have forgotten what it was to desire as a child.

It is a fact that Crabbe habitually uses the Indicative Mood in his work, and that within that Mood it is the Past Perfect tense that dominates, though this tense may contain the Historic Present or the Present of Direct Speech which is set in the past. It is also a fact that this verbial habit logically followed his choice, determined by temperament, of such a plan for a collection of tales as that implied by the title *The Parish Register*. For here the author turns the pages with their registrations of births, marriages and deaths, and then remembers in verse the melancholy, disappointed, shameful stories of those whose names are entered. He turns to a particular past year:

> With evil omen we that year begin:
> A Child of Shame—Stern Justice adds of Sin—
> Is first recorded . . .[2]

---

[1] T. S. Eliot, *East Coker*.
[2] *The Parish Register*, Vol. I, p. 165, of *Poems by George Crabbe* ed. by A. W. Ward.

then the miserable story of the miller's daughter who gave birth to a bastard is dutifully—and admirably—told, for

> Could I well th' instructive truth convey
> 'Twould warn the giddy and awake the gay.

This is truth-telling but is not. By not realizing the girl's desire or slowly-dying hope less than the truth, or even of the half-truth, is told. People are as much what they would do as what they do.

4 WORDSWORTH AND THE MOOD OF MEMORY

The Prelude is an autobiography and so an act of memory. The substance of what is said is not happening simultaneously with its expression. What happens happened in the Past which is "recollected in tranquillity". Immediate enlargement through present discovery is out of account.

The Prelude was written in Wordsworth's middle and late thirties, but its effective experience took place when he was aged seven, eleven and twenty-two and he is to draw on that capital for the rest of his life. Thus, reflective upon past experience, Wordsworth is a meditative or philosophic poet who, having found some great truth, refuses admission of new experience which might discountenance the old. Hence "the unknown modes of being" which were once actively present must remain unknown and become lost save to memory.[1]

The pathos inherent in Wordsworth's achievement can be appreciated by contrasting it with Dante's. As with Wordsworth's great events, the great event in Dante's life had occurred at an early age and was recorded in *la Vita Nuova*. But, *la Divina Commedia*, begun by Dante at just about the same age as Wordsworth began *The Prelude*, while it depends on the tremendous discovery of its author's childhood, does more than commemorate or simply draw on capital. *La Divina Commedia* creates a vast present expansion of the original experience. What happened to Dante at the age of nine continues to grow in him

---

[1] "Imagination has nothing to do with Memory"—a William Blake annotation to the *Poems* 1815 of William Wordsworth. Yet against this we should recall that Aquinas designates Memory an important power of the Soul.

and the growth is forwarded by the act of his poem, and Beatrice comes to mean even more for him in his present and future than she meant in his past. All the tenses and moods go to work in *la Divina Commedia*, and from their working together arises a new tense of a new mood which has no name of the grammarians.

But Dante is exceptional among poets and men. Most of us, like Wordsworth, have little more than memories of subjunctive experience to live on (though Mr. Eliot in *Four Quartets*, under the example of Dante, makes memory the agent of future explorations).

The verbs in the verse of *The Prelude*—and the verbs are all the more prominent because of the general bareness of the verse—reflect the mind or genius of the poem considered as a whole in that their inflexions are overwhelmingly those of the Past Indicative tense: "There *was* a boy . . .", "she *was* an elfin pinnace . . .", etc. Certainly, the Historic Present also occurs in *The Prelude*, and fairly frequently. But we should not be deluded any more than was Wordsworth: the qualifying 'Historic' is significant. Wordsworth was using a variant of the Past, not transmuting it. In *The Prelude* the Historic Present remains historical.

The traffic of Wordsworth's poem is a one-way traffic between his dull *now* and his momentous *then*.[1] There is little over-layering or stratification of tense though there is much comparison between then and now. The memories he chronologically relates form a series whose perspective diminishes at a constant rate as he recalls the milestones of his effective life. But while the 'milestones', those events of his past, severally speak to his *now*, they do not speak with each other. They do not do that because the writer's belief in a progress or development was, despite the evidence of his own poem, too strong. He could

---

[1] Not always a 'dull' now. Fairer to say that the characteristic Wordsworth poem reflects on a 'then' from a 'now' of different quality, as in *Peele Castle* or the lines on *Tintern Abbey. Yarrow Unvisited, Yarrow Visited* and *Yarrow Re-visited* are interesting poems and they are, I have been reminded, relevant to our discussion. But I would rather not write on them here except to remark that the relation between the three is purely a 'calendar' one, as suggested by the dates, 1803, 1814 and 1831. There is comparison between experiences separated by years but no fusion so as to override time. In support of this I would point to the verbial mechanics.

not really impeach his 'present' status once he had proclaimed
that it possessed the consolation of "a philosophic mind".

Yet to be just to Wordsworth, and to distinguish him from
Crabbe, one must recognize that though he is *remembering*, he is
remembering—unlike Crabbe—subjunctives. The boyhood
skating and the prank of the 'stolen pinnace' were indeed
indicative events (and that is their marvel) but these indicative
events were the occasions of vast (but unsaid and so unknow-
able) subjunctive experiences which were/are the real 'stuff' of
the poem, those "unknown modes of being", whose past truth
is the only reason for the poem being written.

But those subjunctive experiences, though still operating and
conditioning "all his moral being", are, almost as much as their
indicative bases, past. They do not happen any more *now*
because youth is an impressionable phase which Wordsworth
is now remembering in "the light of common day". By contrast,
la Divina Commedia (and even *The Four Quartets*) knows, and
makes the reader know, the transmutation of a Past Tense into
the subjunctive of a continuing Present "in and out of Time".

VII Keats: The Subjunctive Realized, or a New Mood

I PRELIMINARY

For Wordsworth the Subjunctive was indeed the genuine Goods. But the genuine Goods were felt, scarcely known, in a Mood of the past, and he had to feed on them in Memory. But for Shelley and Keats the Goods of the Subjunctive were not set in a memorable past but were Possibles. The proper tense for them was therefore a Future, a Future more or less remote. They looked this way → and not, as Wordsworth did, this way ←. And these Possibles were, for Keats and Shelley, more than just Possibles. They were Possibles whose Truth depended on their becoming realized. Without this Belief there was no Hope. On the Belief as well as the Hope that the Subjunctive Goods could—or rather, would—be realized as Indicative depended all, including, of course, the validity of Belief (or Truth) and Hope (the Future) as actions themselves; on this too depended the value of poetry and the worthwhileness of life itself. It must be acknowledged that neither lived to the age of Wordsworth who simply recorded what once was. Yet had they lived to the age of Wordsworth they might have continued to live in hope.

But while both Shelley and Keats believed and hoped that the Subjunctive Possibles were realizable (on the belief rather than on the hope depended the justification of their art and being) yet they were vastly different in their natures or temperaments, as any two men must be the one from the other. And it is this obvious and final difference which explains the specific distinction between the Goods of Shelley and the Goods of Keats. Not only were their specific Subjunctive Goods different, they appreciated them at different ranges. The Future of the one was not the Future of the other. Also the relation between each of the two poets and what they severally desired differed. The distance between himself and the object or state desired diminished through his overtaking pursuit in Shelley; the distance between himself and what he desired shrank, because it approached him, in Keats. Shelley was long-sighted and chased. Keats was short-sighted and it came towards him so that he could smell, taste and touch it. Now this long-sightedness of Shelley and this short-sightedness of Keats (here we speak of the relation between each poet and what he desired as shown in his work—that Shelley was physically long-sighted and Keats short-sighted may, or may not, be relevant) accounts for their individual differences of Tense within the Subjunctive Mood. Moreover each poet shows in his poetry an individual *relation* between his favoured Tense of the Subjunctive Mood and the Indicative. In Shelley the Indicative is disdained and slighted more than in Keats. As for their Subjunctives: Shelley's is pitched in an altogether remoter Future. He envisions the afar off. In his Belief-Hope action it is the Hope component which is the more thoroughly confident. But this will, I hope, become apparent later. Here we are concerned with Keats— though first, perhaps, a word might be offered in explanation of my use of capital letters in this section:

Though mainly agreeing with the practice of the poets we are discussing when they use the relevant words, these capital letters may strike the reader as horribly portentous or pretentious. In Shelley and Keats the usage of capitals indicates the value they gave to certain words and ideas. My usage (above) is justified if, besides serving a precise referential function (so that, e.g., I intend Shelley's meaning of 'Hope' when I write it thus), the initial capital in—say—'the Subjunctive' [1] points to this: in the later Romantics emotional/conceptual *areas* are given a degree (even substance) of reality in excess of what the *names* of grammatical categories, designed for limited purposes, were meant to denote or contain. The

[1] As an adjective or adjectival substantive. For a general policy on this matter, see pp. 3–4.

areas which the categories *could* suggest become endowed with an objective validity. This argues semantic—and other—changes of a nature which this chapter can do no more than suggest.

2   THE GRAMMAR OF ADAM'S DREAM

Shelley, we have said, saw his Subjunctive from afar off and—pursuing it—overtook its futurity in the winged chariot of his poetry. But Keats' Subjunctive, on whose truth and capacity to become indicative truth all depended, came towards Keats or became, in his poetry, borne in on him; to be later born of him.

What took place in his latest and richest poetry Keats had earlier expressed as an article of belief in correspondence:

I am certain of nothing but of the holiness of the Heart's affections and the truth of Imagination—What the imagination seizes as Beauty must be truth—whether it existed before or not. . . . The Imagination may be compared to Adam's dream—he awoke and found it truth.[1]

The claim and the implications are vast. Not only is that which is desired, and, therefore, because 'desired' not yet possessed, 'holy' (though confessedly the term "affections" can refer as much to the desire itself as to the objects of desire), but what the "Heart" so desires it will also possess or find as truth. The organ, which transmutes what is desired into truth, is the Imagination. Each of the two "and's" in the quotation are highly significant. The function of neither is purely copulative. Their meaning can be arrived at by reading for them the mathematical sign of equivalence, viz. =.

Keats, in this letter, is feeling for, and forwards into, his poetic " 'Beauty is truth, truth beauty',—that is all/Ye know on earth, and all ye need to know". That which is desired—and which is to become true—is that which is also beautiful. We have written 'is to become true'. It 'is' to become true because it *must* become true: the quality of belief and desire is such as to render an equivalence between an 'ought to be' and an 'is'.

---

[1] The *Letters of John Keats*, ed. Forman, pp. 67–8. The letter, from which I quote, is dated November 22nd, 1817.

When we say 'ought to be', the reference is not to the realm of moral duty of oughted-ness but to the non-moral realm (if such exists, but to Keats it did) of poetic 'desire'. That which is perceived as desirable, as beautiful, and so prospectively true, is born—because it *must* be born by sheer pressure of desire—into temporal or actual (and what is actual is temporal) existence. This incorporation of desire in the shape of indicative fact is seen by Keats as an *awakening* or real birth. Instead of the delusional intensity of opium-pipe- or beer-dream, or other restricting alternative to actuality, truth exists.

The passage from Keats' letter, affirming a belief in a translation out of a Subjunctive into an Indicative may seem noble but 'preposterous', according to King's use of the word,[1] and absurd. Keats would have been confuted, had he lived, many will think. Some of those who think this might also think that when he died he was less likely to have "outsoared the shadow of our night" into an awakening, that was also a possession of what he desired, than to have passed into oblivion—where he has remained ever since February 21st, 1821—and that, of the three objects he so much desired—"Verse, Fame and Beauty"—only the satisfaction of the first was indicatively known by him. For those who believe such, Keats' letter expresses merely a wish for wish-fulfilment, and his latest and best poems must be read as their author's substitute for carnal possession of Fanny Brawne. But others, along with me, will pray that Keats in death is eternally in a sexual act whose climax is just about to be reached. May that be his continuous ecstasy and the result and reward of his most 'intense' experience on earth! for:

> Verse, Fame and Beauty are intense indeed
> But Death intenser—Death is Life's high meed.[2]

In estimating an act of love, an act of total communion with another human being, as the greatest good the Subjunctive had to offer—greater than 'Verse' or 'Fame'—this side of Death (though he would have such an act sealed by death as his 'Bright Star' sonnet shows), Keats agrees with all the best poets, who were also, possibly, the best men, since the time of the

[1] See p. 113, above.
[2] Concluding lines of the Sonnet beginning: 'Why did I laugh to-night? No voice will tell.'

author of the first part of the *Roman de la Rose*, for whom this experience was the earthly heaven, a terrestial rhyme to the celestial experience of union with God.[1] Yet it would seem, on the evidence of such lines as "Happy love!/ For ever warm and *still to be* enjoy'd! ",[2] that to Keats the moment within the supreme Subjunctive experience was less the moment of orgasm than the moment before. Hence the terms of our prayer! It was the swoon*ing* or the dy*ing*, to allude to the *double entendre* of the Elizabethans with which Keats may well have been aware, not the 'death', that *was* to become—because it *ought* to become, like Adam's dream—true.

Hold the worth of Keats' truth more cheaply who may! and certainly Keats himself let himself in for difficulties and torments, which he had neglected to envisage, when he encountered the pure fact of Fanny Brawne. But it was before he encountered the fact that he wrote the letter, from which we have quoted, while he was scarcely out of the "chamber of Maiden Thought", and he believed his Grammar, and proved his belief, in his early poetry. Certainly, to have to find the matter to fill out *Endymion* strained his rudimentary powers of invention. Nevertheless, the four-thousand-odd lines of this poem were written, and still exist, to state and prove his poetic-Grammatical proposition, viz: that what is desirable and desired enough must/ought to, and so will, become true, and the truth is then an awakening. To do this he has to bring in swarthy Indian girls, and the like, so as to postpone the essential miracle whereby the Subjunctive ought-to-be becomes the Indicative *is*. Yet the shifts to which he is reduced, to eke out his poem, are not purposeless. They contribute to the total meaning. The effect of the dusky Indian girl is not only decorative. When, 'real' as she is, she finally turns out to be one and the same with the blonde and "ethereal" Phoebe, Keats' invention is justified. It is not only essential that the most desired should take on flesh, but it is right that she should be shown to have been alongside Keats/Endymion all the time albeit he knew it not. It is also right that Endymion's mistress should be revealed as non-sectarian in her beauty and gifts. She, with whom union is

---

[1] Cf. "We shall enjoy ourselves here after [*sic*] by having what we called happiness on Earth repeated in a finer tone and so repeated." *Letters*, p. 68.
[2] Italics mine.

desired above all, must be both dusky and moon-pallid; must be earthily warm as well as celestially remote; must be mother-protectress as well as mistress; to satisfy all of Keats and Endymion she must be everything herself. The transformation of Indian Girl into Phoebe is as much a blend as transformation; it confirms an indispensable clause in Keats' Poetic Grammar.

3   THE 'ODE TO A NIGHTINGALE': A NEW MOOD

The most renowned of all English odes can deceive. It can deceive because once having been thought to be extremely 'poetical', because truly dreamy and ecstatic, it is now in danger of being thought 'escapist', adolescent and bad. It is also a dangerous poem to deal with in this book. Though more than any other poem it seems to invite investigation into the workings of the two grammatical Moods, within a single elaborate structure, yet the temptations to simplify are strong. The obvious over-all Verb-Movement of the *Ode to a Nightingale* is *from* an initial Indicative, which is unhappy, *to* a Subjunctive which is intensely blissful. Finally, there is a relapse into, or at least a return to, the Indicative. This is the overall verbial movement, yet a knowledge of this is liable to prevent our seeing the many minute, yet subtle, tensal and modal shifts and variations that occur within these three main divisions.

For though the commencement of the Ode would seem to imply an indicative here-and-now-ness, Keats is other-whither. He would be otherwhere than where he is. True, his heart *does* indicatively "ache" and a drowsy numbness *does* indicatively "pain his sense". But why? because "*as though* of hemlock" he had drunk. The form "As though . . . I had" shows that he is already in the Subjunctive condition, or rather, that the initial Indicatives were framed within a Subjunctive. Something known to be untrue (his drinking of "hemlock" or other "opiate") is taken as having happened in the past[1] and to be the cause of his present indicative state of aching and pain. Already then we have had a hint that if, as A. C. Bradley said, Keats' poetry is "dense", then the density is due as much to

---

[1] "One minute past", but the minute is infinitely expansive or retractable as we all know, and know *consciously* more than ever since the Romantics and largely because of the Romantics.

Modal and, within Modal, Tensal activity as to crush of imagery or profusion of adjectives.

Now hard upon this opening Indicative-within-Subjunctive there comes a genuine passage into Keats' own Intense Present. For the Nightingale is singing in this Tense. Admittedly, by the rules of grammar or logic, both of which would determine from the inflexion '-est',[1] this Tense is an example of the common or garden Present Indicative. Yet I name the Nightingale's tense the Intense Present, a Tense neither of the Indicative nor Subjunctive but of a third Mood, because, *inter alia*, the Indicative is, if anything is, time-bound, and *its* Present becomes Past or Perfect, while—on the contrary—as we know from a later stanza in this Ode, where we are told:

> The voice I hear this passing night was heard
> In ancient days by emperor and clown:

this particular bird's singing has *always* been 'present'. This particular bird is immortal. Yet neither on the evidence of the "sing*est*" of the opening stanza:

> Singest of summer in full-throated ease,

nor from the immediately previous quotation, are we justified in saying that the Mood of the Nightingale's singing is either in the Indicative or the Subjunctive. The singing is not desired, but *is* and yet has always been. Keats introduces us to a Third Mood, a Mood where the desired is indicatively actual and yet is outside of time. So already the first stanza has experienced, and gives us the experience of, the following: the Indicative-within-Subjunctive; the Intense Present.

Having accomplished intricate Modal mechanics in his first stanza, Keats can afford to be simple and assured in his second. Indeed, having come where he aimed to be, he must be simple. In the second stanza the Mood and even the Tense is pure or un-mixed. Throughout, the main verbs are plain Subjunctives of desire: an 'O, that I might have this or that drink so that I could leave this miserable Indicative world and join you in your Intense Present of a Third or New Mood!' is the theme. This is Future-leaning and the stanza itself might well be thin

---

[1] I refer to the passage, " 'Tis not through envy . . . Singest of summer in full-throated ease."

in consequence were it not that these Futures (for all these possibles are, of their nature, yearnings Future-directed) are weighted by a thorough Past. For the Past tense does weight. Consider the pastness of "cool'd" or "beaded". Such words give the flighty Verbs of aspiration and the shameless vocative 'O's' a tradition. All that which is now happening in his new-born Intense Present is also historical and so harmonizes with the 'tradition' that what he hears was heard by those now dead, such as the "emperor", the "clown" or the "Ruth" of stanza VII. All these had heard this Nightingale singing, and in their temporal, as well as spatial, dialects, would have said 'Thou sing*est*'.

Now Keats would join the Nightingale in its Mood, and leave quite forgotten both his actual world of the Indicative (which, as we saw, was yet set within a Subjunctive) *and* his Subjunctive world of mere longing for what *is* not and cannot be. He would:

> . . . leave the world unseen,
> And with thee fade away into the forest dim.

He *would* leave the Indicative world, because it is to be severely judged. It is one where "men sit and hear each other groan"; one where youth "grows pale" and "dies". The Verbs in this stanza do their drudging office in a world where there is no other Mood than what they themselves bespeak. Especially is it a world of Tense, one where Youth, Beauty and Love are continually slipping from a Present reality (of a kind) into the lost reality (of a kind) of the Past. The Subjunctive, from its nature, wishes to escape from this Indicative world of tense (or time) but, again from its nature, can do no more than wish.

It is with the words "Already with thee!", which open the fifth line of the fourth stanza, that the action (or *trans*action) from the world of wretched actuality, combined with a sick subjunctival longing, to the world of the Nightingale, and its life in the Intense Present, is announced as having happened.

As we have seen, the great action, or transaction, of the poem, must be understood to have taken place in the pause or silence between the end of the fourth line and the opening of the fifth line which simply states its news of arrival. The action itself had to take place in this silence because there was no verb to express the action. But, once there—*with* the Nightingale—Keats' verbs, for the remainder of the fourth and the whole of the fifth stanza, are necessarily pure or of one kind. Companioning the bird in its Intense Present, Keats' verbs are in that tense too: the night "is" tender; the Queen-Moon "is" on her throne; and

> here there *is* no light,
> Save what from heaven *is* with the breezes blown.[1]

True, since no inflexions for his Intense Present exist, Keats is obliged to use the inflexions of the common indicative. But this should not deceive us. Since no inflexional forms existed to communicate Keats' experience of habitation in a New Mood —new as far as its creation in verse, or in language at all, is concerned—Keats resorts to poetic periphrasis: an exact poetic re-creation (and definition) of the Intense Present is performed not only by the 'is' forms alone, but by the 'is' forms in combination with all the other elements of the stanzas in which they occur, *plus* the preceding 'action', *plus* a statement of the Subjunctive-conditioned Indicative world from which he has flown.

Keats, we know, *would* seal (or perpetuate) his life in the Intense Present by dying within it, for

> Now more than ever seems it rich to die,
> To cease upon the midnight with no pain
> While thou art pouring forth thy soul abroad
> In such an ecstasy.

But the wish cannot be fulfilled. Not that he will leave the Nightingale (the embodiment of life in the Intense Present) but because the Nightingale will leave him. And that there was this penalty—the penalty of impermanence—attached to residence in the Intense Present is first suggested by the opening line and a half of the sixth stanza:

> and for many a time
> I have been half in love with easeful Death.

For after the fifth stanza he has already ceased to co-exist with the Nightingale in its pure Intense Present. With the sixth stanza he imports into the timeless Mood of the Nightin-

[1] Italics mine.

gale's world the Time, and so Tense, of the world he has left. And in giving a history of his stay in the Nightingale's world, he gives that stay a beginning and in giving it a beginning, he gives it an end. The New, or Third, Mood cannot exist with any other. Keats says he would die *in* this Mood rather than be bereft of it, but since the Nightingale's song is innocent of Time it is also ignorant of Death which, but for Time, would not be. The Nightingale's song simply *is* always, and is as ignorant of deaths as it is of Death.

Having once invoked the temporal 'terms' and inflexions of the Indicative (a strictly 're-actionary' reference) Keats is doomed to become 'forlorn'. He is to be—another 'is'—left behind. The Nightingale, moving on, leaves him behind. Keats is left much as when he began. Not quite, for the experience of a new Mood has intervened. But that experience itself rapidly becomes part of the Time-stream, subject to Tense. This is conveyed by the inflexions of the final stanza. The voice first "fad*es*", but then becomes "buri*ed* deep".

4   TIME AND THE THIRD MOOD

The textbooks of Grammar recognize, in the main, but two Moods: the Imperative forming at most a *quasi* Mood, at worst but a department of the Subjunctive. There is, on the one hand, the plain, tense-bound Indicative reporting actuality and always dependent on inexorable laws of time and space; there is, on the other hand, the Subjunctive which is to contain all lost or living desires and—though these are usually in opposition to the desires—duties, a Mood not subject to tense only because someone or something which is or was desired but not, or not yet, *had*, cannot exist in time; for, if the desire is realized, it becomes subject to time and so indicative. In the poems we have considered, these two Moods are in a state of continual tension. Their history, in poetry, is a dialectic. But the *Ode to a Nightingale*, as I have tried to show, creates, and so defines, a Third Mood wherein desire and possession are both real. Keats creates and experiences this Mood in his poem. His experience is triumphant yet tragic, because neither he, nor "emperor", nor "clown", can abide within this Mood. Human beings can enter this Mood, if they *will* and if they are lucky, but they cannot remain there since human beings cannot avoid reference to the indicative law of time.

Yet Keats, as a suffering man, could not have willingly admitted to the, at least, pathetic conclusion of his poem, the conclusion that knowledge by human beings of the timeless Intense Present could at best be momentary. Indeed, earlier, in his *Ode to a Grecian Urn*, he had attempted to give permanency to a life in his Third Mood. What limited the attempt was the fact that, in this poem, experience of eternal life in this Mood was directly experienced by no 'I'. The experience in the *Grecian Urn* is contemplated, not immediate. 'They'—for it is, consequently, a Third Person poem—who there enjoy life in this Mood are, moreover, but "marble men and maidens". For Keats himself, the life in the Intense Present, of those whose shapes are on the Urn, must remain for him an eternal Subjunctive, not even momentarily possessed as in *Ode to a Nightingale*. Even for the "marble men and maidens", preserved for ever in their Third Mood, there is no consummation of desire. Nor, even, is there the bliss—perhaps for Keats the supreme bliss—of assurance that consummation is certain and imminent. On the contrary, the "fair youth beneath the trees" is in pursuit of a maiden not so near. He has a way to go yet and, when he has made it, a measure of suasion awaits him after that. But Keats can tell him one certainty, and that's no happy one:

> Bold Lover, never, never canst thou kiss,
> Though winning near the goal . . .

For this particular "marble" lover, existing in—and on—the "brede" of the Urn, there is to be an eternity of unsatisfied, or Subjunctive, desire. Even, then, *within* the Third Mood of the whole situation, as it is contemplated by Keats on the Urn, there can exist another Mood in at least one of those involved in the situation, which can act so as to destroy the purity of the Intense Present. As Keats, in the Nightingale Ode, invoked the Indicative Time of his human condition, so the marble youth in the Grecian Urn Ode invokes the Subjunctive: both act on a containing Intense Present so as to destroy it. Human beings can expect an unending life in the Intense Present only after the Resurrection of the Body. On this side of the Resurrection of the Body the Intense Present can be momentarily known, but such experiences can only receive a seal of perpetuity if they happen in "faery lands", and in those lands human actors cease to be fully human.

Now in the *Ode to a Nightingale* we were told that not only people now dead, like the "emperor", the "clown" and "Ruth", had heard the song of the nightingale in "ancient days", but that this same voice:

> oft-times hath
> Charm'd magic casements, opening on the foam
> Of perilous seas, in faery lands forlorn.

In these lines a conjuring trick is wrought by the Verbs. From a remote and pathetic Past the meaning changes—by means of the Participle "opening" and the *quasi*-Verb "forlorn", reinforced by the Adverb "oft-times"—to a resurgent Present: because it often "hath" then it still does, or may do. It is possible for "casements" still to be charmed as it is not possible for dead emperor, clown and Ruth to hear any more. It is dangerous, of course, to put one's trust in faeries or faery lands. But Keats knows this. He knows their existence is a lorn hope while the history of the dead listeners is real. Yet he brings the "faery lands" into the Ode partly because, conventionally accepting their reality, the Intense Present of the Third Mood has a special operancy there, and partly because of the memory of his achievement in *The Eve of St. Agnes* which immediately precedes the two Odes we have just been considering, in the 1820 volume. The three poems thereby form a significantly arranged sequence: graded studies in the Third Mood.

In *The Eve of St. Agnes* the action takes place in a fairyland given just sufficient plausibility by the trappings of medievalism and by the authority of the stanza Spenser had used in *The Faerie Queene*. For this is to be Keats' poem where his dream—like Adam's—comes true.[1] Yet much had happened since Keats had written of Adam's dream. Between that letter and this poem he had left the chamber of "Maiden Thought" and had encountered much actual suffering. The suffering, his reading and his reflection on it, his growth—to give a summary name for many processes—obliged him to transfer the setting for his dream's awakening into truth from an Indicative situation to this hardly-disguised fairyland.

[1] See above, p. 132.

In his poem Madeline awakes from a dream to find the object of her Subjunctive desire a real Indicative. What she most desired was of course, and properly, a young man. So with him she "fled away". But she did so "ages long ago".

Now it is hard, as I think J. Middleton Murry suggested, *not* to be struck by the curiously off-hand bitterness of the last stanza after its first two lines:

> And they are gone: aye, ages long ago
> These lovers fled away into the storm.
> That night the Baron dreamt of many a woe,
> And all his warrior-guests, with shade and form
> Of witch, and demon, and large coffin-worm,
> Were long be-nightmar'd. Angela the old
> Died palsy-twitch'd, with meagre face deform;
> The Beadsman, after thousand aves told,
> For aye unsought for slept among his ashes cold.

Is not the last stanza Keats' criticism of his whole foregoing poem, a criticism springing from the mock-serious tone of the story-teller's conventional "aye, ages long ago"? Yet that is not the whole matter. Certainly, for Keats, love, realized in a person, and become possessed or Indicative, was his supreme— perhaps, finally, only—value. He says that in *The Eve of St. Agnes*, considered as an entire poem. Yet in this stanza he is also saying that a translation from a Mood to a Mood, of a desire into a possession took place, 'so they say' (for this is the tone he gives to a conventional formula by his placing of it), long ago. He scarcely believes it or believes it not at all. The translation of Mood, which is the matter of the poem, is too good to be true except—except in a "faery-land". Already, in this stanza, all "faery-lands" have become forlorn.

Yet we have seen enough to realize that not only is there an enormous and fateful working of Tense and Mood in the poetry of Keats, but that it was Keats who first in English poetry most genuinely defined and created a Mood, and a Tense within it, unrecognized by formal Grammar.

VIII Shelley and the Future Tense

I SONNETS WITHIN ODE

IF there is one poem of Shelley's which on examination reveals not "a general mess of imprecision of feeling",[1] but, on the contrary, an exact feeling communicated through a superb control of technical resources, then we have a reason for supposing that other of his poems, similarly studied, might show the same organized excellence. Especially we might be hopeful of those longer poems written from 1819 onwards to his death.

In the *Ode to the West Wind* there is much activity going on between the various parts. Thus, besides the intricate pattern of sound-rhymes (or rhymes in the accepted sense of the word), there are 'rhymes' of image and 'rhymes' of theme. And these image-rhymes and thematic-rhymes are incremental in effect, and are consistent with the poem's development. Yet, the poem as a whole is completely characteristic of Shelley in tone and temperament and in its direction.

But we must have it before us.

Ode to the West Wind

I

O Wild West Wind, thou breath of Autumn's being,
Thou, from whose unseen presence the leaves dead
Are driven, like ghosts from an enchanter fleeing,

Yellow, and black, and pale, and hectic red,
5   Pestilence-stricken multitudes: O thou,
Who chariotest to their dark wintry bed

---

[1] T. S. Eliot, *East Coker.*

143

The wingèd seeds, where they lie cold and low,
Each like a corpse within its grave, until
Thine azure sister of the Spring shall blow

10 Her clarion o'er the dreaming earth, and fill
(Driving sweet buds like flocks to feed in air)
With living hues and odours plain and hill:

Wild Spirit, which art moving everywhere;
Destroyer and preserver; hear, oh hear!

II

15 Thou on whose stream, mid the steep sky's commotion,
Loose clouds like earth's decaying leaves are shed,
Shook from the tangled boughs of Heaven and Ocean,

Angels of rain and lightning: there are spread
On the blue surface of thine aery surge,
20 Like the bright hair uplifted from the head

Of some fierce Maenad, even from the dim verge
Of the horizon to the zenith's height,
The locks of the approaching storm. Thou dirge

Of the dying year, to which this closing night
25 Will be the dome of a vast sepulchre,
Vaulted with all thy congregated might

Of vapours, from whose solid atmosphere
Black rain, and fire, and hail will burst: oh, hear!

III

Thou who didst waken from his summer dreams
30 The blue Mediterranean, where he lay,
Lulled by the coil of his crystalline streams,

Beside a pumice isle in Baiae's bay,
And saw in sleep old palaces and towers
Quivering within the wave's intenser day,

35 All overgrown with azure moss and flowers
So sweet, the sense faints picturing them! Thou
For whose path the Atlantic's level powers

Cleave themselves into chasms, while far below
The sea-blooms and the oozy woods which wear
40 The sapless foliage of the ocean, know

Thy voice, and suddenly grow gray with fear,
And tremble and despoil themselves: oh, hear!

IV

If I were a dead leaf thou mightest bear:
If I were a swift cloud to fly with thee;
45   A wave to pant beneath thy power, and share

The impulse of thy strength, only less free
Than thou, O uncontrollable! If even
I were as in my boyhood, and could be

The comrade of thy wanderings over Heaven,
50   As then, when to outstrip thy skiey speed
Scarce seemed a vision; I would ne'er have striven

As thus with thee in prayer in my sore need.
O, lift me as a wave, a leaf, a cloud!
I fall upon the thorns of life! I bleed!

55   A heavy weight of hours has chained and bowed
One too like thee: tameless, and swift, and proud.

V

Make me thy lyre, even as the forest is:
What if my leaves are falling like its own!
The tumult of thy mighty harmonies

60   Will take from both a deep, autumnal tone,
Sweet though in sadness. Be thou, Spirit fierce,
My spirit! Be thou me, impetuous one!

Drive my dead thoughts over the universe
Like withered leaves to quicken a new birth!
65   And, by the incantation of this verse,

Scatter, as from an unextinguished hearth
Ashes and sparks, my words among mankind!
Be through my lips to unawakened earth

The trumpet of a prophecy! O Wind,
70   If Winter comes, can Spring be far behind?

We notice that the poem is both an ode and sonnet sequence. This in itself is remarkable because ode and sonnet sequence would seem to be forms of different, in fact conflicting, intentions. The ode requires a subordination of its constituent stanzas in favour of a grand overall effect; but the sonnet sequence, composed of short poems written over a period of time, is linked together only by theme or the personality of the writer, and each sonnet is often too resistant to submission to an overall structure for the sequence to have a recognizable form of its own. So Shelley has here made his five sonnets do something exceptional in making them subscribe to an ode. The result is too successful to allow us to say that the nature of the sonnet is thereby distorted. Rather, Shelley has simply made a unique addition to the sonnet's uses and capacity.

But that the sonnets do what they do—subdue themselves to a larger design—in Shelley's Ode is to be attributed largely to the *terza rima* in which each sonnet—and so the whole poem—is written.[1] The effect of *terza rima* (when handled with a respect for its special capabilities) in the sonnet is to liberate it from the Shakespearean interaction of three quatrains (three parallel similes) plus couplet; or alternatively, considering the Miltonic variety, to liberate it from its tendency towards an arc of slow swelling to climax at the end of the octet—the climax forcing some kind of counter-movement in the sestet. A liberation of the sonnet from both the Shakespearean and Miltonic modes was essential to Shelley's purpose. His purpose, besides needing speed, demanded of each sonnet an ability to 'run on' to the next one in the series.

At the same time, regarding Shelley's poem as an ode, the *terza rima* has a clear advantage over couplet or alternating rhyme (each of which creates its characteristic pattern of pause or punctuation), considering the impulse towards a rapid sweep combined with a sense of interlocking unity.

The whole poem's peculiar assurance and rapidity essentially follow from a breaking down and reconstitution on different lines of the sonnet. The means, through which this reconstitution is achieved, is *terza rima*, and we must assume Shelley's perception of the possibilities of this system. Each sonnet now moves in triplets instead of in quatrains (or larger units), and these triplets are interlocked through rhyme. Moreover, the first three sonnets are linked, in their entirety, through a com-

[1] That Shelley, among English writers, is the great master of *terza rima*, has been observed by Mr. Eliot.

mon final rhyme. And then, supporting the interlocking of sound-rhyme is the scheme of interlocking imagery.[1]

2 POEM AND PRAYER

The poem is both ode and sonnet sequence. It is also a prayer. For this we have Shelley's explicit admission in lines 51–2.

Attempting to understand the nature and structure of prayer, we can say that a prayer follows a formula; that it employs certain elements and that these elements occur in an almost invariable order. These are (i) An Invocation of the name of the Person or Power to be addressed; (ii) A Listing of that Person's or Power's superior or divine attributes (with the intention that He, She or It should be propitiated or flattered by the recital, and reminded of His, Hers or Its capacity to grant a petition); (iii) A Confession by the suppliant of his inadequacy and failure unless he is divinely aided, and (iv) a Petition. To this we should add that in a prayer of some length, as in Shelley's poem, the initial Invocation continues to punctuate the remainder at intervals calculated to prevent the attention of the Person or Power from wandering. It will also be understood that the elements enumerated, while always occurring, can be of varying length and importance in relation to each other.

Now applying this formula to Shelley's poem, we can say:

That the Invocation occurs in the four opening words of the poem, and that this Invocation thereafter punctuates the poem in lines 13 and 14, and at the end of lines 28 and 42;

That the Listing of the West Wind's attributes is the substance of sonnets I, II and III; and that

The Confession appears in IV, lines 54–5; and that

The Petition follows in IV, and is developed in V.

3 SONNET, PRAYER, IMAGE

Shelley's poem is at once, then, ode, sonnet sequence and prayer. While some of the resources which it draws on for its elaborate organization are obvious, they must now be mentioned

---

[1] The imagery of the poem is interpreted by G. Wilson Knight in his fine essay on Shelley in *The Starlit Dome*, see especially pp. 200–7.

in a conspectus whose partial aim is a demonstration of the dynamic rigour of Shelley at his best.

The second stage of his poem (the four stages of the order of prayer do not coincide with, but do not conflict with, the formal division into sonnets), namely, the Listing of the attributes of the West Wind, is carefully developed: sonnet I lists the attributes of the West Wind when its prowess is displayed on land; sonnet II lists what the West Wind can do, and does, in the sky; sonnet III deals with the activity of the Wind on—and under— the surface of the sea.

Throughout this stage the Wind is apprehended as both "destroyer and preserver", and as a force whose destructive and creative activity gradually becomes co-extensive with the universe, even encompassing it. Progressively the dual result of the Wind's action is sharpened in consciousness. This dualism is to be resolved in sonnet V, but by that time the West Wind has grown from being merely a meteorological phenomenon proper to autumn (though his reaction to it as that was Shelley's starting point[1]) into something very much more.

It should be noticed that while sonnets I, II and III deal with the activity of the Wind on the levels of land, air and sea, respectively, yet they all share in the image of the "leaves". In sonnet I they are the actual "leaves" of the earth's trees. In II, the "loose clouds" are "like earth's decaying leaves". In III, the "oozy woods" of the ocean bottom are despoiled of their leaves. But the image of the "leaf" does not end there. In IV Shelly wishes to be "as a leaf" or, what has become its equivalents, "a cloud", "a wave"; and in V he is as a "forest" with "falling leaves". Thus the "leaf" is an incremental image which transcends both the formal divisions into sonnets and the divisions exerted by the prayer formula.

Indeed the significance of the poem rests largely on the result of the continuity, open or concealed, with which the images of tree and leaf are sustained right through.

---

[1] "This poem was conceived and chiefly written in a wood that skirts the Arno, near Florence, and on a day when that tempestuous wind, whose temperature is at once mild and animating, was collecting the vapours which pour down the autumnal rains. They began, as I foresaw, at sunset with a violent tempest of hail and rain, attended by that magnificent thunder and lightning peculiar to the Cisalpine regions"—Shelley's note.

4 PREPARING TO ASK

We turn from a view of the poem's parts, its form, structure, and its percurrent image, to a consideration of each sonnet.

In I, following the opening Invocation, there is a series of three images. To each of these the West Wind is likened. First, the Wind is like an "enchanter" driving "ghosts" (3). Since the leaves are dead it is appropriate that they should seem like ghosts. Next, the Wind is like a "pestilence" (5), for the leaves in their discoloration, are like "multitudes", already contaminated, streaming from a plague-striken city. Finally, the Wind is like a "charioteer" (6) which is driving "wingèd seeds" (an echo, perhaps, of Plato's winged *steeds*). All three of these images *for* the Wind's action, on the level of the earth, create a sense of vehement flight and pursuit (and are thus typical of the main body of Shelley's imagery elsewhere in his poetry). They will also have their 'rhymes' in II and III, for this stage of the prayer is constructed on a system of three parallel statements. Meanwhile, however, the images in question have already established the Wind as a "destroyer" (14). But now the precipitation of the meaning, as of the movement of the verse, begins to slow (after 6). This retardation, to an almost still centre in the flurry of violent movement, is to be balanced by a corresponding 'death' passage in II. In I, seeds lie "cold and low" (7), and are like "corpses" (8). But they are to be "preserved", for Shelley is already beginning to apprehend a poetic solution to his Death/Life problem. The seeds wait until the counter-movement (for there is to be more "driving", though from another direction) is initiated by the spring wind. This azure Wind will "blow" its clarion. This is happily ambiguous: a wind "blows" and a clarion "blows" (and the meaning blows = blooms is not far away). But the "wind-clarion-blowing" complex is not confined to line 10, for by the time we reach the second half of this rhyme, which closes the Ode (69–70), the "clarion" or "trumpet" has developed an enormous increment of meaning and suggestion which it dispenses back to the image in I. In lines 69–70, the analogy to the Last Trump of Christian revelation is clear (for that Trump is also the herald of life born out of the condition of death, and like the Ode's is to be heard in the future). Already, by the time that I ends with its

Invocation, the West Wind is something more than a seasonal gale.

The second sonnet is both enlargement and parallel. The West Wind's action in the sky is simultaneous with its action on the earth. Its behaviour there is destructive as on the earth. What it destroys is similar: the "loose clouds" are like "decaying leaves" and the clouds are stripped from their "boughs". This is an image-rhyme which refers forwards as well as back since the "stream" (15), the "Ocean" (17), the "blue surface" (19), as well as the action of shaking (17 cf. 42) anticipate IV. Meanwhile, the "angels" now rhyme with "ghosts", and the "Maenad" with the "charioteer".

These image-rhymes are followed by II's rhyme to I's statement of death (7, 8). But now instead of just the "seeds" being entombed like corpses, it is the whole of nature that is 'sepulchred' and "vaulted" over by the Wind's minatory vapours (24–27). The dejection, which is associated with the year's—and Shelley's—decay and dying, from which, however, new life is to come, grows and deepens through each formal stage of the poem until the 'turn' is effected. By the end of II the year is dead, or dying: even so the Wind will inflict on it the punitive fierceness of "black rain", "fire" and "hail".

In III (the action of the West Wind on—and under—the sea) there is a change of mood, though the image-rhymes of I and II are sustained. As in I and II there is a passage of stillness in the midst of violent movement but, instead of coming three-quarters of the way through the sonnet, it comes at the beginning, and is more developed in preparation for the langour of IV. The structure of III relies on two parallel impressions of the Wind "waking" the sea, and the rhythm is one from stillness to flurry in place of flurry to stillness. The movement is that of a lyrical reverie. Shelley is drawing on blissful memories instead of foreseeing the future. Here are "dreams" not "visions", providing an introduction to the autobiographical element of IV. The "summer dreams" of lines 29–36 suggest that peculiarly rarefied and limpid gaze which Shelley (most "spiritual", i.e. most body-abstracted, of poets) exercises when he is happy. He is happy because the weight of attention is on these delicate Mediterranean "dreams", and not on the "wakening". But in the second image, from line 38, this emphasis is changed. Now the attention is on the Wind's vast corrugation of the Atlantic. Speed returns with the *l* and *p* sounds of line 36, and harshness with the combinations of *cl* and *ch* in "cleave" and "chasms"; and the thematic rhyme returns with the image of the "sea-blooms and the oozy woods", on the ocean bed, turning "gray with fear" and being despoiled of their "leaves".

By the end of III, with its movement from stillness to movement, running counter to the movements of I and II, a stage of the prayer is completed. By listing the Wind's attributes in a widening focus, he has praised and propitiated and is now ready to ask. Not only is the Wind 'softened up' enough to be asked, but Shelley too is in the right psychological state *to* ask. We now see the West Wind *through* Shelley's spirit. For this state of affairs (the poem's—and our—readiness to turn to the petitionary element in the order of prayer) something is even due to such a line as

> So sweet, the sense faints picturing them !

Superficially the line may seem bad, but it serves as an advance signal for the I (Shelley)—Thou (West Wind) relationship of IV.

5   ASKING

In the petition, lines 43–5 have the force of 'Oh, if only I were' or of 'If only I *could* be ('be' rather than 'have') this or that'. Thus his petition is, at first, in tune with human craftiness in that he does not ask directly but instead voices his wishes aloud in the expectancy of being heard by one who should by now be a benevolent listener. And his wishes, also at first, are humble enough. He wants simply to become "as a dead leaf", or "cloud", or "wave". These are references to the whole contents of I, II and III, respectively. He is asking merely that he also might be part of the process of decay, destruction, death and—and so by implication—new life. Next, following the formula of prayer, he interposes his confession of weakness and dependence. So Shelley is devoid of virtue, bowed by time, and is in "sore need".

After this humble confession Shelley becomes much emboldened. In V, the mere hinting aloud of wishes now behind him, he can *demand* his deepest desires with increasing confidence. And as his confidence increases so the object of his desires—his demands—increases. In line 58 he asks to be not merely like a dead leaf but like a whole "forest". The relation between the West Wind and Shelley is also changing and growing rapidly closer. He can request the Power to make him its lyre, i.e. the instrument through which it is to sound. Later (61), the mounting demand reaches its culmination in:

> Be thou, Spirit fierce,
> My spirit! Be thou me, impetuous one!

The previously dejected suppliant is now content with nothing else than actual union or identity with the great Power addressed, while still remaining its instrument, so that the West Wind, through him—but it now indeed *is* him—shall "awaken" the earth. His poetry is to be as the seed-bearing leaves.[1]

Shelley has not quite done yet. For in the last three lines of his Ode (for clearly the five sonnets have submerged their personalities into one large poem of elaborate organization), there is a final demand:

> Be through my lips to unawakened earth
> The trumpet of a prophecy!

This echoes the "clarion" of I. The "clarion", in I, was to "blow . . . o'er the dreaming earth" in spring. Here "spring" is also present (70), but it is a more comprehensive sort of spring which is to awaken. There is, as remarked before, a suggestion of the 'Last Trump', but Shelley prevents this from being too strong since it is his own form of apocalypse that he is prophesying.

6   THE ACTION OF HOPE

Analysis shows that the *Ode to the West Wind* has a concentrated system of interlocking of sound- and image-rhymes, an interaction of parts within a whole, and a controlled development. These are virtues that have been denied to Shelley. Yet the poem is thoroughly representative of its author in imagery (of

---

[1] Leaves, dead or living, do not bear seeds. But Shelley's mistake is not deeply relevant.

natural forces—winds, waves, clouds—all in precipitate movement and pursuit), in pitch, in its visionary quality, and in the
nature of its 'message'. It is a fair supposition that other late
poems of Shelley, such as *Adonais*, *The Triumph of Life*, or
Epipsychidion, even *Prometheus Unbound*, might—if examined—
reveal a similar cohesion.

No wonder therefore that his imagery is always, in Dr.
Leavis's phrase, "leaning forwards". This has been taken as a
reproach but, in fact, in thus "leaning forward" the imagery
becomes exactly mimetic of the Aristotelian 'action' of the poem
which is Future-directed. As for the diction: an understanding
of Shelley's nature, as one which involved a detachment from
his Present, in favour of the Future of his vision, explains the
remoteness of his language from human actuality.[1] He was not
so much 'abusing English' as using a variety for his special purpose, a variety which sought as big a remove as possible from
the experience of a past-governed Present. Hence, too, the
general avoidance of human and social imagery, with its
historical connections, in favour of the volatile imagery of
nature which, under Shelley's will, is 'speeded up', and races
forwards-inclined. Similarly, Shelley's rhythms in their un-
inhibited speed and impetuosity enact the course of Shelley's
will towards his Future.[2]

The degree of dependence of Shelley's apocalypse on late-
eighteenth- and early-nineteenth-century anarchical or revolutionary theory, based on Rousseau's doctrines of human perfection, can be exaggerated. Indeed, the relation between
Shelley, on the one hand, and Platonism, Rousseau, the French
Revolution and Godwin, on the other, is not one of dependence.
Shelley's poems are less reflective of the climate 'of opinion' of
the age in which they were produced than creative of that
'opinion', and of the age's thought and feeling. It is through
Shelley's temperament and its natural 'action', as willed in his

---

[1] Sir Herbert Read's study of Shelley's personality (*In Defence of Shelley*)
is not only interesting in itself but is valuable in that its findings reflect back
into the poetry.

[2] Prince Marinetti, the founder of Futurism, appropriately celebrated the
centenary of Shelley's drowning in the bay of Spezia with an aeroplane and
speed-boat display.

poems, that we can perceive the climate of his age. Revolutionary slogans are *used* by Shelley as instruments of a poetic purpose, and in being used, their meaning is expanded beyond their original denotation. They become, in the context of Shelley's poems, *signs* for a universal human perception of an ideal condition of joy.

It is for this reason that Christian revelation and doctrine provide as good a commentary on Shelley's Ode as the works of Godwin or Rousseau. One can apply to the destiny of the "wingèd seeds" (7), the inference derived from the words "Unless a seed fall into the earth and die . . .", etc. Similarly, the analogy of the spring "clarion" (10), and the "trumpet of a prophecy" (69) with the 'Last Trump' of the Christian myth has been noted. Here are cases where Shelley is using ancestral Christian *signs* not so much deliberately as inevitably. These are perhaps details. But the Ode throughout, and as a whole, in its tracing of Shelley's characteristic contour, or action, and in its comprehension of death as an indispensable condition for the realization of a state of new life, exerts a resemblance to Christian orthodoxy to such an extent as to make any attempt on our part to overstress the resemblance of Shelley's 'thought' to that of his generation perverse. For, to use Christian terminology again, Shelley's poem, and his poetry generally, in seeking a desired state of joy, posited in the future but apprehended in the instant, exemplifies—as no other poetry in English does successfully (for Hart Crane's nerve failed)—the act and virtue of Hope, a confident expectancy of what is desired coming to pass, whose tense of course is the Future. Romantics, it is said, disregard human limitations. But it is of the nature of Hope to act in despite of a recognition of human limitations, and

> to hope till Hope creates
> From its own wreck the thing it contemplates.

Now it is natural that Shelley whose poems are preeminently acts of Hope written in the Future tense should have turned to Dante as he did. It is easy to make a ludicrous contrast between nineteenth-century Platonic idealism and medieval scholasticism, in favour of the latter. But if Shelley is no mere versifier of the one, neither is Dante of the other. Both transmute and transcend the doctrines to which some critics would wish to confine them as translators; and both, as Mr. Eliot said of Shelley, "had to a high degree the unusual faculty of passionate apprehension of abstract ideas".[1] More important perhaps than even these similarities—and at least as binding as the differences of time and language were dissevering—was their shared obligation, based on a similar 'committed' avidity of temperament, to 'imitate' the action of Hope.[2] They both trace the movement of the soul from its state of dejection *now* to a joy located in the future and which is apprehended, through poetic vision, as immediate—even though the *signs* for Dante's 'action' were those of Christian Paradise, and the *signs* for Shelley were those of a Godwinian millennium.

It is also true that the *signs* for 'the ineffectual angel's' millennium were poorer than the *signs* for Dante's Christian Paradise, though the dependence of Shelley's millennium on a diffusion and re-application of Dante's signs cannot be ignored. As we have seen they are present in the Ode. But the integrity of the passion of Hope outgrew the efficacy of *signs* even when they were at their perfection in Dante. That these *signs* have been further weakened since Shelley, even as the virtue of Hope has declined, may be demonstrated by putting beside this stanza of *Adonais*:

> The One remains, the many change and pass;
> Heaven's light forever shines, Earth's shadows fly;
> Life, like a dome of many-coloured glass,
> Stains the white radiance of Eternity,
> Until Death tramples it to fragments.—Die,
> If thou wouldst be with that which thou dost seek!
> Follow where all is fled!—Rome's azure sky,
> Flowers, ruins, statues, music, words, are weak
> The glory they transfuse with fitting truth to speak.

an ironical paragraph from Graham Greene's *Brighton Rock*:

"Our belief in heaven", the clergyman went on, "is not qualified by our disbelief in the old mediaeval hell. We believe", he said glancing swiftly along the smooth polished slipway towards the New Art doors through which the coffin would be launched into the

---

[1] *The Use of Poetry and the Use of Criticism.*

[2] I am using the Aristotelian terms 'imitation' and 'action' as interpreted by Francis Fergusson in his brilliant and seminal book, *The Idea of a Theatre.*

flames, "we believe that this our brother is already at one with the One." He stamped his words, like little pats of butter, with his personal mark. "He has attained unity. We do not know what that One is with whom (or with which) he is now at one. We do not retain the old mediaeval beliefs in glassy seas and golden crowns. Truth is beauty and there is more beauty for us, a truth-loving generation, in the certainty that our brother is at this moment reabsorbed in the universal spirit."

which is as much a blasphemous parody of the Hope of Shelley as it is an exposure of the insufficiency of liberal-Platonic-post-Darwinian 'Christianity'.

Dante and Shelley shared the Future Tense action of Hope. Dante's signs were much healthier, the *termini* of his action extended further both ways, and he had a considerably longer life than Shelley in which to write. But it is their comparable action that explains the serious devotion of Italians to Shelley to this day, rather than the facts of his residence in that country or his death off its shores. Unlike Dante and Shelley, English poets concentrate, in the main, on *this* City, here and now, rather than on the next.

The spiritual kinship involved a technical stimulation. Shelley learned from Dante how to 'keep his eye on the object'. He also learned that *terza rima* was the keenest instrument for the writing of a poem with a sustained religious theme.

IX *Later Shifts and Developments*

I PURE SUBJUNCTIVE

WE saw that Keats, from a base in the Indicative, made pioneering, though short-lived, settlements in the Subjunctive, that he believed (as though his poetic life depended on it, which it did) in those settlements with the intensity necessary for their becoming true; that, in becoming true, they became, though for a moment only, Indicative. Those moments, in possessing simultaneously the qualities of Subjunctive and Indicative, define a Third or New Mood. In Shelley, the Future Conditional was more real than any indicative for it was the tense in which To Hope and, for Shelley, to hope was to live. He lived in hope.

Poets of the late 1820's, the 1830's and early 1840's, form a group. I think of Thomas Hood the Elder, George Darley and Thomas Lovell Beddoes. Despite the rich individuation suggested by the labours of Professors C. C. Abbott, H. W. Donner and Edmund Blunden, they have much in common.[1] Eminently what they have in common is a mechanism of the Verb. Inheriting the various Subjunctives of such poems as *Christabel*, *Kubla Khan* or *Eve of St. Agnes* (and combining their experience of these with a view of Elizabethan dramatists, and a view of themselves as neo-Elizabethan Dramatists), they initiated their poems within a Subjunctive entirely free from Indicative circumscription and from all but the barest Indicative reference. The 'action' of their poems lies in a continuous and increasingly remote penetration within the same Mood.

[1] They are considered as a group in Mr. J. Heath-Stubbs' stimulating study, to which I acknowledge a general indebtedness, *The Darkling Plain.*

Yet there is no testing and breaking of limits such as we know in Jacobean drama because in the pure Subjunctive there are no limits. Nor can there be.

Yet a cover formula can never be just to individuals, and in the case of Thomas Hood the Elder, it might be argued—of his 'serious' poems as of his 'comic'—that his work is not so much shrouded in the Subjunctive as that it is ignorant of the frontiers between Subjunctive and Indicative or even, to give it a fresh status of interest, that its motive is to dissolve those frontiers. But it is rather more likely that the questions Hood raises in the following stanzas issue less from an intention to exploit a confusion of the categories of Mood in poetry, than from a genuine puzzlement, or bewilderment, as to where "dreams" or "fictions" begin, and end, and a wonder as to the distinction between 'thought' and indicative 'act':

> Some dreams we have are nothing else but dreams,
> Unnatural, and full of contradictions;
> Yet others of our most romantic schemes
> Are something more than fictions.
>
> It might be only on enchanted ground,
> It might be merely by a thought's expansion;
> But, in the spirit or the flesh, I found
> An old deserted Mansion.[1]

Because of the liquidation of some frontiers, Hood—in or out of the body—reaches the deserted Mansion and by some compulsive force enters it and, like a somnambulist, he mounts the stairs and is drawn to enter a room where some terrible crime or sin, probably a murder, *might* have taken place. All this latter part is related—woodenly, creakingly, at a relentlessly even pace—in the Past Indicative. But the poem, at the beginning, was so firmly set in a Subjunctive dubiety that the poem's meaning scarcely remains contingent on whether what it relates actually happened.[2] And this is as fair a ruling of *The*

---

[1] *The Haunted House.*

[2] Hood's contemporary in America, E. A. Poe, would seem highly relevant to the discussion here. Certainly Poe explored, and perhaps broke down, frontiers between Moods. Yet I exclude him from this section because of his closer relations with two other literary traditions than with our own. One would just indicate here that the temporal—in practical Grammar, tensal—shufflings in Poe, accompanying the dissociation of one sense, e.g.

Dream of Eugene Aram (was the murder dreamt or committed? or did the dream actualize itself?), and of *The Last Man* and other 'serious' poems as of *The Haunted House*, whilst in his Comic poems Hood had a licence—as had Edward Lear—to play with the Subjunctive of Nonsense.

In the person of Lycus (in *Lycus the Centaur*) Hood professes his disinclination to believe in an Indicative:

> Who hath ever been lured and bound by a spell
> To wander, fore-doomed, in that circle of hell
> Where Witchery works with the will like a god,
> Works more than the wonders of time at a nod,—
>
> At a word,—at a touch,—at a flash of the eye,
> But each form is a cheat, and each sound is a lie,
> Things born of a wish—to endure for a thought,
> To last for long ages—to vanish for nought,
> Or put on new semblance?

But before we too hastily condemn Hood's weakness of 'will', or the weakness of these lines, we should compassionate the poets of Hood's time on their situation. Third-generation Romantics, with no public and members of no society, they could not say 'We' or think it. Each was as Hood's centaur, Lycus, an outcast, forced to deploy his powers within his solitary Subjunctive realm.

Darley is likewise a First Person Singular, an 'I' poet. With *Kubla Khan* and Keats' and Shelley's poems much in his mind, he aims to convey opposed Subjunctive states of bliss and dejection—states of an extreme bliss and misery, entirely individual (however keen or dull any man's sensibility is, it is his own), and without reference to any Indicative or outward conditions which might have provoked them. In Darley there is no acceptance of the Indicative, still less an effective conciliation of this Mood with the Subjunctive and a resulting emergence of a Third Mood—as happens in Keats. On the contrary, though he may not have been aware of the great difference between himself and Keats which this implies, there was not for Darley even a straight choice between Indicative

sight, from another, e.g. hearing, which under his influence enter French poetry, made their appearance in English poetry this side of the Atlantic before Baudelaire began to write.

and Subjunctive. Hence there was no possibility of *translation* from one Mood to the other; still less of a habitation in a Mood born of a process beyond translation. For Darley the Subjunctive alone existed as the area in which poetry ought to be written, a Subjunctive isolated from contact with all his Indicative life. He was less like Keats in his poetry than he supposed.

Yet Darley, who was a mathematician of parts, was conscious of the folly of trying to *live* within the exclusively subjunctive area in which he thought poems ought to have their being. This is apparent from the early *Errors of Ecstasy* where the swooning Mystic, who would prefer oblivion to the 'this' of actuality:

> Annihilation, dark and everlasting!
> Why this were well, I could exchange for *this*,

is told by the Sage not to be such a damn fool.

In *Nepenthe*, Darley's finest poem, there *was* to have been the same warning. Of the intended scheme for the poem, he wrote:

Canto I attempts to paint the ill effects of over-joy, Canto II attempts those of excessive melancholy. Part of the latter object remains to be worked out in Canto III, which should likewise show —if ever I could find confidence and health and leisure to finish it —that contentment with the mingled cup of humanity is the true Nepenthe.

Yet though the glory of the state of "over-joy"—its fine symbol, the Phoenix, is consumed by its own fire—is short-lived and the Canto ends with the 'I' of the poem (Darley) falling from giddy heights because of his mind's "insane misprision", and though the inadequacies of the state of "most majestic sadness" are exposed, there is no sign of the intended Canto III, which was to have counselled moderation and acceptance of the Indicative, ever having been actually written. It looks as if, whatever he had intended to write, Darley could not—when he came to it—reject those states which had his imagination's approbation as being solely the condition of poetry. Though, at the end of Canto II, he sinks down to his "calm, dear, humble soil", he does so to become one with "nothingness". Not trying to be unkind, this suggests that he did not sink low enough.

Nepenthe on the one hand, and *l'Allegro* and *Il Penseroso* on the other, make a significant contrast. Milton's poems on two opposed states of soul are set against an observed landscape whereon actually-observed persons move. The opposed states of soul are controlled by an indicative world.

This section has so far dealt with the most sheerly depressing phase of English poetry. Sad it is that men so gifted as Beddoes, Hood and Darley (Beddoes, especially, was mightily gifted) should, on the basis of premises—premises either no longer valid or from which they personally could not proceed—inherited from their predecessors, the Greater Romantics, have felt chosen to speak each in his private Subjunctive language without reference to their actual world. But their failure, if what they accomplished should be adjudged a failure (in which case *Death's Jest Book* is so depressing because it is so magnificent a failure), is as much a reflection on their literary and social situations—that it is possible to speak of these 'situations' as separate, is itself an indication of a wider failure —as in themselves. These situations condemned each of them to the isolation of his private Subjunctive.

Yet the early Tennyson had been as confined within his own Subjunctive as Beddoes, Darley and Hood were within theirs. We say 'confined', for to be free of a territory with no limits whatsoever, and to be free of that one territory only, is to be as 'confined' as to have the run of some other single territory where boundaries are fixed and intransigent.

But it is a measure of Tennyson's greatness that his poetry, from 1842 onwards, structures itself on the Indicative Verbs governed by the pronoun 'we'. The Indicative Verb and the pronoun seem at first assumed rather than felt. Later, those for whom he claimed to speak—perhaps persuaded by the claim— owned that he did so speak. Yet the plain, confident statements of the Indicative Verbs in *In Memoriam*, and in other poems, habitually receive qualification or muted denial from their dependent Subjunctive clauses. At other times, more subtly, the Indicative statement is half withheld by the Subjunctive rhythm to which it is set. Tennyson created a rich *semantic* orchestration by continuously challenging the assertions of his framing and sustaining Indicatives by his internal and half-concealed Subjunctives.

2   T. S. ELIOT: THE EXTREME OF GRAMMAR

More so than in the work of any other English poet the problems raised or discussed in this little book are implicit in the poetry and plays of Mr. T. S. Eliot. Several have been subjects for discursive treatment in his prose. The problems, signalized by the grammatical terms of Tense, Mood and Preposition, are problems of Time, of the Timeless, of Relation. But dependent on these are further problems which can be grouped under such headings as: Problems of Action, Being and Possession (concerns of the Active Voice; concerns of the verbs *to be* and *to have* whether self-sufficient or serving as Auxiliaries); of Agency and Suffering (Pronoun as Subject and Pronoun as Object); of Purpose, Desire, Hope, Moral Compulsion (the Subjunctive Mood); of Relations Actual, guaranteed by the senses, as when two persons are in one room (place for the literal Pronoun) and Relations Subjunctive, as when the persons are divided by space, time or death (the metaphorical Pronoun).

Now to estimate the importance, the pressure and urgency of these problems, in Eliot's poetry, dramatic and non-dramatic, as revealed, for example, by the choice of pronouns and the tenses of (to select at random) such lines as:

> He who was living is now dead
> We who were living are now dying[1]

is altogether beyond the scope of a Primer. All that I can here hope to do is to hint at the richness of material awaiting other students of Mr. Eliot's poetic grammar, to give one or two instances myself later, and meanwhile refer, though in shorthand, some of these problems, as they exist in Eliot's poetry, to his discursive prose and to post-Tennysonian development of thought regarding Time (expressed by verb-inflexions) and personality and personal relations (whose instruments of denotation are the Pronoun and Preposition).

In *Tradition and the Individual Talent* we were told that "the historical sense involves a perception, not only of the pastness of the past, but also of its presence". The words "past" and "presence" denote here, as always, time—time which is particularized in language by tense. It is fair to say that Eliot's

---

[1] *The Waste Land*, 328-9.

dictum, and its poetic manifestation in *The Waste Land*, reflects —though it partly anticipates—profound changes in our general conceptions of time (and so of space, and so of the time-less, and so of relations in—and outside—time and space) since, say, Tennyson—though Tennyson too anticipated changes.

Anthropology, Archaeology and Pre-history, Einstein's Theory of Relativity, Joyce's application of Vico's philosophy, the shortening of distances by means of modern methods of transport and communication, recent Psychology and Biology have all worked so as to alter, not only our former time- and space-scales (inasmuch as the human record is seen to be much, much longer; terrestial space has shrunk; celestial space has expanded so greatly as to be as defeating to conception as that former 'infinity' which it is not) but the whole structure of our minds. Such an alteration would seem to require a development of grammar—and of linguistic mechanics generally—to match the structural alteration of the mind. For, except by periphrasis, or by an allusiveness such as that of the lines from *The Waste Land* quoted above, how else can we communicate our aware-ness, occasional or pressing, that time is not, or is not only, sequential? that all parts of the past are still present, commune with each other, and simultaneously co-exist with our *present*? We have no single Tense as yet to express this awareness, though *The Waste Land*, which is a stage and a summation of a long series of the author's poems in which a realization of both the order and simultaneity of events in time becomes progressively more inclusive and complex, communicates it by its Grammar, whether structural or by the inflections of detail.[1]

If the Grammar of the earlier poems, no less than the plain statements of the critical essays, reveals a living and habitual preoccupation with the indicative time and times, past and present, of history, then the plays, the later poems, and eminently *The Four Quartets*, concern themselves with this (and these) in their relation to the timeless.

---

[1] English is rich in strong verbs, e.g. *run-ran*; *sing-sang-(sung)* etc. It seems to me strange that Wilfred Owen, who wrote one or two *great* poems and gave promise of many more in his development and exploitation of para-rhyme, never, or rarely, if at all, made para-rhymes from such resources. Using the *ablaut* of strong verbs he would have been able, one might think, to strike chords in which Present and Past commingled and contrasted.

There is first the timelessness of the Subjunctive might-have-been, a fictitious event, since it never took place, but which still has a living reality *of a kind*:

> What might have been and what has been
> Point to one end, which is always present.
> Footfalls echo in the memory
> Down the passage which we did not take
> Towards the door we never opened
> Into the rose-garden.[1]

The two halves of the first line, referring to two kinds of reality, though only the second is 'actual', seem to be given status equal in importance. That there are thus two kinds of reality, co-present, and not one, is entirely due to the truthfulness of that 'not' in the fourth line and the succeeding, and consequent, 'never'. But of the undeniably sad, almost desperately sad, kind of continuing reality of the 'might-have-been', we were told earlier that it is an 'abstraction':

> Remaining a perpetual possibility
> Only in a world of speculation,

which lines define clearly the Subjunctive histories of all men at all times as known here in the history of one man.

The earliest of *The Four Quartets* struggles to say the problem, and successfully in the light of its Poetic Grammar, of the relation between Indicative and Subjunctive existence. The later *Quartets*, also engaged with the relation of events in time with the quasi- or para-events in the timeless, reach the only solution possible. And the only solution possible was, and is—for the Incarnation is both a past historical and a continuous event—the only solution actual. The Incarnation was/is an event/possibility at once both Indicative and Subjunctive:

> Here the impossible union
> Of spheres of existence is actual,
> Here the past and future
> Are conquered, and reconciled.[2]

though to "apprehend", as distinct from it being given one to momentarily perceive, "the point of intersection of the timeless

---

[1] *Burnt Norton.*   [2] *Dry Salvages.*

With time" is an occupation, we are told, reserved for the "saint"—or the saints.

The vocations or offices of the poet and the saint may be analogous; they are not identical.

3 THE GRAMMAR OF DANTE INTO ENGLISH

I began the previous section by saying that the work of no other English poet was so occupied by the problems implied by the forms of Verb-inflexion, Pronoun and Preposition as was the poetry of T. S. Eliot. The qualifying epithet was deliberate. Most of the best English poetry is primarily concerned with the earthly city and its fluctuations in time. It is no less great for that: but, in Italian, Dante (and he is really singular in this respect, whether the rest of Italian or the the poetry in other modern European languages is considered) is as intellectually and passionately curious about, and concerned with, the heavenly city as he was with Florence. Therefore, besides Florence, he was concerned with two other city-states: one of them was temporal like Florence, yet perfect; the other, like Paradise, eternal.

La divina Commedia, from the nature of its scheme and design, involves and enforces a manipulation and control of tenses and Mood and Voice such as no other poem has quite had to face. Whatever the conditions of being (whether temporary in Purgatory, final in Hell or Paradise) forming his immediate subject at any one juncture in the poem, Dante simultaneously has to carry in mind, in his own and in his reader's, other states of being—present, past and to come. He is the supreme explorer of Subjunctive states of soul as they anticipate or follow actual deeds.

Intensively as he creates his sense of multiple 'times', reverberating in accord or discord with the particular tense-inflexion he happens to be using at the moment, Dante, in the last canto of his poem, answers the challenge to do something yet harder: while still using grammatical inflexions he dissolves the sense of time, which hitherto has been of prime concern, so that it no longer exists in his (yet temporal) contemplation of the Beatific Vision. Here other categories of Grammar have simultaneously to be surpassed. He ceases to be pronominally distinct from God

(Three Persons in One God) and from Beatrice in her enjoyment of God.

It would appear that from *Ash Wednesday* to the Quartets and the plays, Eliot has increasingly learnt and assimilated the Grammar of Dante. His cross-transference of much of that Grammar, and his application of it, with some individual proper differences, to the poetry of another language, English, means, among other things, that the Grammar of previous English poets is open to be seen afresh as in a new light.

X *Preposition in Poetry and Translation*

I RELATIONS ACTUAL AND METAPHORICAL

A PREPOSITION, the *Shorter Oxford English Dictionary* tells us, is "one of the parts of speech . . . serving to mark the relation between two notional words, the latter of which is usually a substantive or a pronoun; as sow *in* hope, good *for* food, etc. The following substantive or pronoun is said to be 'governed' by the preposition."

Accepting the root idea that Prepositions denote the relation between person and person, between person and thing, between thing and person, between idea and person, between person and idea, between idea and thing, between thing and idea, or idea and idea (or any of these in the plural), etc., we can well agree that Prepositions can be as significant in situations of poetry as they can be in situations of life.

This is obvious, but to have an example:

Iago: Why, that he did: I know not what he did.
Othello: What? What?
Iago: Lye.
Othello: With her?
Iago: With her? On her: what you will.
Othello: Lye with her? Lye on her? We say Lye on her, when they be-lye-her. . . .[1]

That, in Othello's imagination, Cassio topped Desdemona, and because he topped her he tops her presently (the Tense of

---

[1] *Othello*, IV. 1. 33-7.

the Verbs, in the passage quoted, moves from Past "did" to Present "lye") means—of course—that to him the final stage of a relation has been, or is now again being, reached. Progressive stages of a physical relation from the "with" to the "on" is denoted by these Prepositions, and in the shortest possible way. For a lover can be *from, by, with, under* or *on* his mistress. If he is far *from* her he is yet disposed *for* and *to* her. If he is lucky enough to be *with* his mistress, he yet hopes to get *on* her. But to be *on* her he must be alone with her for he can be merely *with* or *beside* her in public.[1] Yet we must bear in mind that Prepositions are not confined to denoting the physical relation between bodies in space. A man can write to his mistress from afar declaring that he is *near* or, even, *with* her, etc. When the man writes this, means it, thinks it real, then his Preposition is less an instrument of, than an actual metaphor. Prepositions have their life in Subjunctive desire as they do in Indicative actuality.

We have instanced a case where Iago by 'mounting up' his Propositions can make Othello take the opposite course—fall down in a trance of agony. It shows that Prepositions are effective and can be effectively used by Iagos. Along with other elements—images, rhythm, Tenses of the Verbs, syntax[2]—Prepositions can be profitably studied in a poem and conclusions drawn from the manner in which they do, or do not, work.

2 PREPOSITIONS AND TRANSLATION

But the task generally indicated by that last sentence is altogether huge. Here, it is practicable only to select two pieces of verse, whose acquaintance one has earned, and which are not too formidable. One of these pieces is my own. I know its demerits and am not shy of them. Moreover, I have deliberately chosen it because it is not an 'original' poem but a para-translation (or paraphrase). It was made immediately after the experience of its original, a Swedish poem which I hoped not only to render, but also to advance or mutate. I choose this

---

[1] One is still keeping within the terms of Othello's imagination and, according to Eric Partridge (*Shakespeare's Bawdy*, p. 24), Shakespeare never conceived of a man lying underneath in the act of copulation.

[2] The contribution of syntax towards the meaning of a poem has been ably demonstrated by Donald Davie in *Articulate Energy*.

para-translation and its original precisely because prepositional usage is highly individual to a language. Even momentary reference to English and, say, French idioms will prove this to be so, and, for this reason, I shall so stretch my remarks on Prepositions as to include remarks on translation—in so far, at least, as they relate to the 'translation' of this particular poem.

My original runs as follows:

Riddar Stig's fall[1]

Konungen talade till Riddar Stig:
"Du skall nu föra min fana uti krig."
Riddar Stig ridar inför vallen.

"Huru skall jag föra din fana så tung,
5   min häst är för liten, och jag är själv för ung.

Huru skall jag föra din fana så blå,
min häst är så liten, och jag är själv så låg."

Riddar Stig rider sig över en äng,
efter komme fienden som nederfaller rägn.

10   Riddar Stig rider sig inför en sjö,
efter föllo fienden som nederfaller snö.

Riddar Stig rider sig över en bro,
efter kommo fienden som fallande flod.

Konungen talade till Riddar Stig:
15   "Du släpp neder din fana och värj ditt unga liv."

"Det skall aldrig spörjas i mitt land,
det jag skall släppa fanan utur min egen hand.

Det skall aldrig spörjas till vår by,
det jag skall släppa fanan med skammen till att fly."
20   Riddar Stig rider inför vallen.

Riddar Stig rider sig över en ö,
efter föllo fienden, de slogo honom till döss.
Men nu ligger Riddar Stig slagen.

---

[1] From Ek and Blomberg: *Svenska Folkvisor*, (Stockholm, 1938, p. 71); a seventeenth-century Swedish poem of which an earlier version is found in Danish. Though Riddar Stig was a historical figure, the subject of the poem (which was danced while it was sung) namely, a fallen hero lamented over by girls and women, was of course widely distributed in the European tradition. See Appendix II.

25 Som de finge veta Riddar Stig var död,
efter honom gräto så mången fru och mö.

De lade Riddar Stig uppå högan bår,
fruer och jungfrur de krusa hans hår.

De lade Riddar Stig i svartan mull,
fruer och jungfrur de offrade gull.
30 Men nu ligger Riddar Stig slagen.

My 'translation' goes:

Rider Stepp's Fall

The king spoke up to Rider Stepp:
"Carry my banner into the war's deep."
Rider Stepp rides out into the valley.

"How shall I carry your banner so hung,
5 My horse is so little, myself so young?"

"How shall I carry your banner so blue,
My horse is so little, myself so low?"

Yet Rider Stepp rides himself over a plain,
And the fiend comes after in a squalling rain.

10 Rider Stepp rides himself over a ford,
And the fiend there meets him in a boiling flood.

Rider Stepp rides himself over a sea,
And the fiend comes after in a howling snow.

The king spoke up to Rider Stepp:
15 "Sleep under my banner and hold your hope."

Said the Rider: "Never in this land
Shall your banner be rent from out my hand.

It shall never happen, while I am by,
That the banner be taken, or with shame I fly."
20 Rider Stepp rides out into the valley.

Rider Stepp rides himself over an island,
And the fiend came after and the fiend was violent,
And now lies Rider Stepp slain.

When it came known that the Rider was dead,
25 They wept for him many, both women and maids.

They laid Rider Stepp upon a high bier
And women and young women dressed out his hair.

They laid Rider Stepp down in dark mould,
And women and young women they offered him gold.
30   But now lies Rider Stepp slain.

Note on Prepositions

line 3 inför = before > into[1]

The Swedish preposition *inför* is used to express as wide a diversity of relations, probably wider, as the English *before*. For example, 'he came *into* the King's presence' might be rendered 'han kom inför konungen'. But *inför* is also used to convey the meaning of 'in front of' ('in the fore of') as it does in line 3 which is literally rendered 'The Knight Stig rides before the wall'. (That line 3 is a refrain and so signals a different Tense from the strophe is a thing to comment on, if at all, later.) This becomes, in the translation, "Rider Stepp rides *out into* the valley" because of the English noun governed. It was not just a case of Dr. Johnson's "sheer ignorance" that caused the turning of *vallen* (= the wall, rampart from Latin *vallum*) to *valley*. Partly responsible was the power of early memory's "Into the valley of Death/ Rode the six hundred", perhaps, or later memory's Biblical "Yea, though I pass through the valley of the shadow of Death, yet shall I fear no evil", or Bunyan's echoes of this. Partly responsible only: for there was a deep need to *invert* the reared-up Latin *vallum* so that it became the depressed Latin *vallis* in order that the Myth of the Pursued Man might be engaged. The Pursued Man goes out, or away, from Walls that terrify as well as guard and then goes down, and away from, into the safety (the false safety) of the valley. A fastness is on a mound, and he must go away from it, and, in going away from it, he goes down. Stepp, in going down, goes "into" (2) a depth to find a war of which he might be ignorant, while Stig, in the original, differently—for it is a difference of planes—had gone out into the war (*uti*, 2), which is (surely) gone out *to* war, and so had gone out (and to it) on the level. In the Swedish, once below the fortress, there are no geographical contours to heed in the poetry.

[1] On each side of the mathematic sign for 'equals' = are the nearest literal equivalents. The sign > is intended to mean what the literal equivalent becomes (or is changed into or grows into) in the English version.

line 8 över = over, remains (with difference) over

That Swedish *över* = English *over* and so should be rendered 'over' might seem over-obvious, for in English it is quite natural to say 'a man rides over a plain'. But by retaining in translation the original's reflexive "rides himself", the motion of the rider in relation to the plain becomes different, the horse now takes long semi-magical leaps, instead of trotting, and the horseman has a *preternatural* horse.

line 10 inför = up to (i.e. as far as) > over

In the original the Knight rides "up to" the (edge of the) lake. But, turn *sjö = lake* into *sea* (the need for a dissonant to *snow* also invites this) and follow into English the implications of the reflexive verb of this and the adjacent strophes, and then certainly Stepp no longer trots "up to" the sea-shore, as the edge of the lake has become, but he must go *over* the sea— riding. His horse is already preternatural and now, with its Rider, does this demonic act. It is necessary, in myth, that the demonic should participate.

lines 9, 11 som nederfaller rägn . . . som nederfaller snö = as down pelts rain . . . as down falls snow > in a squalling rain . . . in a howling snow

It might be objected that in the prefixial *neder* = down, the adverbial notion overtops the prepositional. That may be so, but the prepositional is there, disguised as prefix, and must be dealt with.

The original creates simple parallel similes: the *human* enemy pursues the banner-bearer as relentlessly and as steadily as rain or snow descends, respectively. But the Swedish *fiende = enemy*, when he is rendered as "Fiend" (making him thereby supernatural), demands that his pursuit should be more than 'as' or 'like' something else. If an ordinary man can pursue like rain coming down then the Fiend must do more, viz. habit himself *in* the rain, or vest himself *in* the snow. Then indeed he will *come after*, for the drops and the flakes fall slantwise. Pursuing, because of Him inside them, the rain and snow no longer fall vertical. They slant after Stepp.

line 12 över = over

Same observations apply as to the *över* = over of line 8, except that (owing to exigencies of rhyme, etc.) by rendering *bro* = bridge, not as 'bridge' but as 'ford', something happens to maintain and intensify the poetic logic of the 'translation'. Ordinarily, one rides *over* a bridge but *through* a ford. But if one rides *over* a ford then one does what other people cannot do: otherwise a ford would hardly be necessary. One is then an exceptional rider or on an exceptional horse. Stepp and his steed can fly or leap over a ford if they can ride over a sea. Moreover, by leaping the 'ford' he evades, or overreaches, the Fiend who has now become or has inhabited the "boiling flood" (for this change from the original's simile the same observations apply as to the changes in lines 9, 11) thinking surely to collide with Stepp broadside, thinking not to be *sur*-passed.

line 15 neder = under > under (?)

In the original the King threatens Stig: "You let slip the banner (i.e. you let go of the pole supporting the banner), and beware your life!" This is far from my rendering "Sleep under my banner and hold your hope". I cannot defend my rendering, quite apart from any crass bungling which confounded 'slip' with 'sleep'. By preserving the idiomatic *neder* and rendering it literally as *under* nothing is gained, an opportunity is lost. The failure of the English couplet must be attributed to an unlucky rush at the preposition in the original. A lucky rush would still have gone straight to *neder* as the key to the situation but would have brought back a different result.

line 17 utur = out of > from out

The gaff, the mis-fire or failure to fire, over *neder* in line 15 is to blame for another failure here. Stig declares (literally): "Never shall it be noised about in my feof (which I hold of you) that I shall relinquish the banner out of my own hand." But my rendering of 'out of' as "from out" transfers the stress *from* the subjective determination of the hero *to* the objective force of the enemy-wrencher. This is wrong because our eager hopes should be with—and in—Stepp (yes, we should be still *in* Stepp), until he disappoints us by his death. Here, in line 17, we in him should still have high hopes in (and of) him.

line 20 inför = before > out into

In this, the last statement of the first refrain, Stepp is far away in his journey and is still advancing. He is not, thanks to the behaviour of the prepositions in the act of translation, still prancing or boasting before (in front of) the castle *wall*.

line 21 efter = after > for

In Swedish one weeps, longs or mourns *after* someone or something (e.g. "as pants the hart after cooling streams") whereas in English one weeps, longs or mourns *for* someone or something. The difference is deeply expressive of the difference between the minds of the two peoples. In Swedish one would follow the object of desire or grief to be where he is. In English one would have him come back to the place which he has left. But I have substituted one *idiom* for another, though it might seem right that Stepp, in death, should be pursued by the tears of women as he was pursued, in life, by the Fiend. But, where *physical* relations are concerned, the women and maids are weeping *over* Stepp as he lies on the bier and some such prepositional contrast (implying stillness after the movement of *after*) might have been better.

line 26 uppå = up on > upon

It would have been stronger to have dared the divided 'up on'. Then each syllable, then the separate meanings of 'up' and 'on', would have been given consecutive weight. In my "upon" the compound sounds are lightened and the word loses the full meaning of either component. Stepp should certainly have been laid 'up on a high bier'. Whereas he had sped down and along 'and all along down' (as in *Widecombe Fair*) he should now be horizontal, high-up and motionless. The stage direction for the *tableau* set is muted by the "upon".

line 28 i = in > down in

Whereas Stepp had moved himself through many lateral obliquities, he can now only *be* moved vertically. After his high uprearing on a bier he is put down into a deep grave. The addition of "down", in the English, emphasizes the movements of the Pursued Man, dead or alive, and refers back to the "Fall" of the title. (In the Swedish title *fall* = death, and so refers simply to one event within the poem; in the "English Fall", more widely, refers to the context of the death as well as to the death itself.)

3   PREPOSITIONAL ENERGY

From the foregoing comparison of two series of Prepositions in two poems, or in two phases of one and the same poem, certain findings emerge. For, while Prepositions in any kind of verbal communication, are highly important because, as Formal Grammarians put it, they "serve to mark the relation between two notional words", yet their function in poetry is particularly interesting because there it is in their power, beyond their *marking* of known ones, to *discover* new relations. For instances of this, compare lines 9, 11 and 13 in the two versions.

But while the discovering-force of the Preposition, as a marker or maker of relations, is everywhere potentially tremendous, its energy is, perhaps, particularly discernible in two kinds of poetry, viz. (i) *caroles*, *visor*, and other early genuine dance-poems, and (ii) drama.

To confine ourselves to considering the force of the preposition in the first kind.

These poems being memorized, spoken and heard, and not read, have a simple boldness of diction and a simplicity of syntax. Convoluted constructions and thick, gorgeous, 'Keatsean' adjectival and adverbial components would have muffled hearers' understanding of what the poem was, or what it was about. But their simple diction and their insistence on the natural order of words encourage Prepositions to a particular daring. Moreover, early popular poetry focusses on physical deeds and movements. Images of the bodies of men and women are strong in it. These images changing physical or emotional relations with respect to each other, or with respect to the landscape, charge such words as *with, from, to, even, through, up, down* with fateful responsibility. Yet again, and perhaps most important of all, poems in this class were not only sung but were danced, and in being danced we must suppose the movements of the performers to be strongly, boldly *mimetic* of what the words conveyed and of the poem's Aristotelean action. The force of the Prepositions just listed would be revealed in performance of the poems.[1]

4 PREPOSITION AND TENSE

While the main purpose of this section has been a brief demonstration of the function of Prepositions, it is in order to say something also about the Verbs in the poems we have been discussing, since this might help to underscore some of the points we made elsewhere, or to add to them.

Tense :

It will be noticed that the Tense of the two refrains, viz.:

Riddar Stig *rider* inför vallen.
and
Rider Stepp *rides* out into the valley.

and

Men nu *ligger* Riddar Stig slagen.
and
But now *lies* Rider Stepp slain.

is that of the Present Indicative and therefore contrasts with the Tense of the body of the poem which, following the mode of narrative, is in the Past,[2] while the Tense of the direct speech, since it is expressive of intention, is in the Future.

Why? and what is the poetic result of these differences of Tense?

The Knight Stig was, as we have said, a historical hero, and the deeds of this real man, charged with carrying the King's banner, are *remembered* in the *visa*. The correct Tense of memory is, of course, the Past: Stig lived, carried the royal banner, did his deeds (however incompletely remembered, or however exaggerated by folk-memory) and then died—all in the past. And that explains the dominant Tense of the poem.

But, to turn to the direct speech, this narrative poem *includes* drama. Within the memory of the past, the King and Stig

[1] The truth of these observations should be tested with reference to the poem 'He bare hym up, he bare hym down' which is quoted and analysed above, pp. 20-35.

[2] A tensal contrast, between the refrain and the body of the poem, exists in 'He bare hym up, he bare hym down'.

become *dramatis personae* and speak for themselves. They give their commands, say what they *will* do, and threaten. When this happens (in lines 2, 4–7, and in the uninterrupted dialogue of 15–19), we, whether dance-poem performers, or danced poem audience, or readers re-creating, pass back into the time remembered, become *of* the time of the hero, when his deeds were still *to* do (not yet *done* to be reported), and experience his hopes which, like all hopes, lie in the Future.

So far, then, we have an overlaying of two times, a ← of memory and a → of hope (largely subjunctive) though the length of the shafts of both arrows is livingly distensible or protractive.

Yet the refrains are in the Present, in a kind of Present that is peculiarly a resource of poetry. Stig who lived, fought or fled, and died in past time continues to 'ride' *and* continues to 'lie' dead. "Naturally so!", it might be urged, "since he 'rides' *and* 'lies' in death whenever the *visa* is performed or whenever a performance is re-vived in reading or memory." That is true, though the 'real' Stig is dead and will never have his choices or his chances again. But, living then in that kind of 'life' or 're-living', he takes on the quality of a Myth with possibilities of development merely hinted at by the present English version. Apart from, and yet with the help of the Prepositions, we see in the *visa* a co-operation of Past, Future and Present Tenses in a single short poem. Much of the poem's worth arises from this co-operation.

Appendices

THE 'Hill' version, given on p. 21 ('*The Grammar of Two Poems*'), occurs on 165b of Balliol MS. 354. This was the Commonplace Book of one Richard Hill, who describes himself as "servant with Mr. Wyngar, alderman of London".

The MS. is described by E. K. Chambers and F. Sidgwick as "a miscellany of the widest character containing English, French and Latin, poems, romances, fabliaux, extracts from Gower and Sir Thomas More; receipts, legal notes, London customs, etc." The items were entered over a period from before 1504 to *c.* 1535. From evidence of style the composition of "He bare hym up . . ." appears to antedate its transcription by Hill by about seventy or eighty years.

The 'Hill' version was first *printed* by Flügel in his *Neuenglisches Lesebuch* in 1895 (see Chambers and Sidgwick, *Early English Lyrics*). It was first adduced as a parallel to the Staffordshire version (see below) by Sidgwick in 1905 (*Notes and Queries*, 10th S., IV, 181). The Balliol MS. was edited as a whole for the E.E.T.S. by Roman Dyboski in 1907.

On p. 21 I have followed convention by substituting 'w' for 'v', 'th' for 'y', 'and' for '&'.

In 1807 James Hogg published *The Mountain Bard*. In this collection occurs a poem, "Sir David Graeme", which includes the line

The dow flew east, the dow flew west,

on which Hogg offers a footnote:

178

I borrowed the above line from a beautiful old rhyme which I have often heard my mother repeat, but of which she knew no tradition, and from this introduction the part of the dove naturally arose.

Hogg sets down the "beautiful old rhyme" as follows: (It was first contrasted with the 'Hill' and the Staffordshire versions by Dr. Edith C. Batho in *The Ettrick Shepherd* in 1927.)

> The heron flew east, the heron flew west,
> The heron flew to the fair forest,
> She flew o'er streams and meadows green,
> And a' to see what could be seen;
> And when she saw the faithful pair
> Her breast grew sick, her head grew sair;
> For there she saw a lovely bower,
> Was a' clad o'er wi' lilly-flower;
> And in the bower there was a bed
> With silken sheets, and weel down spread;
> And in the bed there lay a knight,
> Whose wounds did bleed both day and night;
> And by the bed there stood a stone,
> And there was set a leal maiden,
> With silvere needle and silken thread,
> Stemmyng the wounds when they did bleed.

The version by Hogg on p. 21 above appeared in the course of his narrative poem, "The Bridal of Polmood" (*Winter Evening Tales*, Vol. II), 1820. Lines three to six inclusive of the earlier version disappear and the poem is now given a spuriously archaic spelling. Hogg, on this occasion, gives no indication that the poem is not of his own original composition (see Batho, *op. cit.*, and also Kenneth Richmond, *Poetry and the People*, pp. 152–8).

The Staffordshire 'version' was sent by a correspondent, signing himself 'ε. τ. κ.', to *Notes and Queries* (3rd S., ii. 103) in 1862 with the note:

The following Christmas Carol was sung, to a singular wild and beautiful tune, by a boy, who came to my house as one of a company of morris-dancers during the Christmas season some years ago. I took it down from the boy's dictation; he said he had learnt it from his father, and had never seen it written or printed. It was in North Staffordshire.

The Staffordshire Version

Over yonder's a park, which is newly begun,
  All bells in Paradise I heard them a-ring;
Which is silver in the outside, and gold within,
  And I love sweet Jesus above all thing.

And in that hall there stands a bed,
  All bells in Paradise I heard them a-ring;
Which is hung all round with silk curtains so red,
  And I love sweet Jesus above all thing.

And in that bed there lies a knight,
  All bells in Paradise I heard them a-ring;
Whose wounds they do bleed by day and by night,
  And I love sweet Jesus above all thing.

At that bedside there lies a stone,
  All bells in Paradise I heard them a-ring;
Which is our blessed Virgin Mary them kneeling on,[1]
  And I love sweet Jesus above all thing.

At that bed's foot there lies a hound,
  All bells in Paradise I heard them a-ring;
Which is licking the blood as it daily runs down,
  And I love sweet Jesus above all thing.

At that bed's head there grows a thorn,
  All bells in Paradise I heard them a-ring;
Which was never so blossomed since Christ was born,
  And I love sweet Jesus above all thing.

'ε. τ. κ.'s request for information respecting the "ballad" (as he called it), and the tune to which it was sung, went unanswered until Sidgwick's conjecture in 1910.

In the *Journal of the Folk-Song Society*, IV, a correspondent, J.A.F.M., conjectures that the 'wounded knight' and the 'fawcon' of 'Hill' and the 'hound' of the 'Staffordshire' implies a common relationship with the *Three Ravens* and the *Twa Corbies*.

---

[1] "How is this line to be amended?" was 'ε. τ. κ.'s query.

APPENDICES

The Derbyshire Version

This version and its tune were noted down by Ivor Gatty and R. Vaughan Williams in 1908 from a rendering by a carol-singer at Castleton, Derbyshire. Words and tune were printed in 1910 (*Journal of the Folk-Song Society*, IV).

Down in yon forest there stands a hall,
The bells of Paradise I heard them ring;
It's covered all over with purple[1] so tall,
And I love my Lord Jesus above anything.

In that hall there stands a bed,
The bells of Paradise I heard them ring;
It's covered all over with scarlet so red,
And I love my Lord Jesus above anything.

At the bedside there lies a stone,
The bells of Paradise I heard them ring;
Which the sweet Virgin Mary knelt upon,
And I love my Lord Jesus above anything.

Under that bed there runs a river, (?flood)
The bells of Paradise I heard them ring;
The one half runs water, the other runs blood,
And I love my Lord Jesus above anything.

At the foot of the bed there grows a thorn,
The bells of Paradise I heard them ring;
Which ever blossoms since He was born,
And I love my Lord Jesus above anything.

Over that bed the moon shines bright,
All the bells of Paradise I heard them ring;
Denoting our Saviour was born this night,
And I love my Lord Jesus above anything.

The above gave rise to an elaborate discussion on the various 'versions', by Miss Annie G. Gilchrist, in the same number of the *Journal of the Folk-Song Society*.

1 "Distinctly 'purple and pall' when sung to me."—Dr. R. Vaughan Williams' note.

The Staffordshire and the Derbyshire 'versions' seem to me to be clearly related to 'Hill', though both the former have been reduced to the status of Christmas Carol when, with the passage of time, this came to be the only kind of carol admitted. Such a 'reduction' involves a corruption and loss of the original poem's meaning.

2 'RIDDER STIGS DØD'

THE Danish *Ridder Stigs Død* (see above, p. 169) is a much less exciting poem than the later Swedish *Riddar Stigs fall*. It starts very similarly:

> Kongen taler till Ridder Stig:
> "Og du skalt føre mit Banner i Strid."
> Men Ridder Stig han maa sig ej!
> (The King speaks to the Knight Stig: "And you shall carry my banner in battle." Refrain: But Rider Stig he meets with harm.)

but instead of leading the hero through a mythopœic landscape, it leads him through a series of eleven two-line battle-stanzas concluding with the death of Stig still pertinaciously gripping the banner. (The actual Stig Hvide did indeed fall at Viborg in 1151 during the dynastic wars between the kin of Valdemar and the kin of Magnus.) The king comforts Stig's betrothed by offering her Karl the Rich as a husband. The girl refuses this offer of a substitute, declaring that no one can equal in worth the dead Stig.

Some of the battle-stanzas have a good ring:

> Der fløj Pile saa tykt som Hø
> Igennem Ridder Stigs Aerme rød,
> (There flew arrows as thick as hay Through Rider Stig's red sleeves.)

or

> Der fløj Pile som brendendes Brand
> Igennem Ridder Stigs hvide Hand,
> (There flew arrows as burning fire Through Rider Stig's white hand.)

but, as with comparable battle-piece images in, say, *The Battle of Otterbourne*, the reader's delight depends on the novelty and boldness and yet precision of simile. Obviously the *vise's* parallel similes for thickly-flying and piercing arrows are surprising *and* more precise than the unoriginal 'blood'-simile in *Otterbourne*:

> They swakked their swords, till sair they swat,
> And the blood ran down like rain.

but the delight is limited to the delight from a newly-perceived relation. Their function is the function of 'closed', as opposed to 'open', detail. That is, their value is entirely local; they do not, like an 'open' image, spread (as a running stain spreads) a glamorous significance over the entire poem. Nor do they suggest an area outside the poem altogether.

From *Ridder Stigs Død* to *Riddar Stigs fall* marks a gain in suggestiveness. In the later poem the 'fiend' has come into his own; the death of Stig arouses the grief of all women-kind (he is as their son to all married women; as the father of their children-to-be to all young women) not simply the sorrow of his betrothed. What had been, in the Danish version, a series of stanzas, to be added to at will, has become a dramatic structure with two well-defined and well-balanced movements.

Stig Hvide (to be distinguished from the later and politically more important Stig Marsk, also celebrated in verse) is also the subject of another pair of poems whose theme is the magical one of the casting of runes in order to induce love. But the runes, mis-directed, operate on a woman other than the one he intended.

Index